55
50¢

D1606352

DATE DUE

Dn MAR 1 0 '80			
GAYLORD			PRINTED IN U.S.A.

GETTING AND SPENDING:
The Consumer's Dilemma

This is a volume in the Arno Press collection

GETTING AND SPENDING:
The Consumer's Dilemma

Advisory Editor
Leon Stein

*See last pages of this volume
for a complete list of titles*

THE FOLLY OF
INSTALMENT BUYING

Roger W[ard] Babson, 1875-1967

ARNO PRESS
A New York Times Company
1976

Editorial Supervision: EVE NELSON

———◆———

GETTING AND SPENDING: The Consumer's Dilemma
ISBN for complete set: 0-405-08005-0
See last pages of this volume for titles.

Manufactured in the United States of America

———◆———

Library of Congress Cataloging in Publication Data

Babson, Roger Ward, 1875-1967.
  The folly of instalment buying.

  (Getting and spending)
  Reprint of the ed. published by F. A. Stokes, New
York.
  1. Instalment plan. I. Title. II. Series.
HF5568.B24 1976   332.7'43   75-39241
ISBN 0-405-08006-9

44,303

THE FOLLY OF
INSTALMENT BUYING

THE FOLLY OF
INSTALMENT BUYING

By

ROGER W. BABSON

Author of
"If Inflation Comes," etc.

FREDERICK A. STOKES COMPANY
NEW YORK   MCMXXXVIII

Printed in the United States of America

DEDICATED

TO

CARL BULLITT RANTERBERG

A PIONEER

IN

CONSUMER BUYING

PREFACE

Three reasons make Instalment Buying a subject of white-hot interest to every family with a reasonable intelligence-quotient.

(a) Victims of the instalment industry are not confined to the foolish virgins who sign the mink-coat contracts. Part of the burden of this subversive system is strapped on the backs of cash customers. This comes from trading with merchants who themselves are loaded with instalment contracts for store fronts, store fixtures, delivery trucks and other equipment. When paying the excess prices, necessitated by instalment-ridden stores, you are giving a financial blood transfusion to the instalment industry. This is true even though your signature never touches their dotted lines.

(b) Desperately our economists, statesmen, bankers and industrialists are hunting for grease for the screeching and stalling machinery of our modern economic system. That bunch of oily waste, known as instalment-payment plans, is handy and tempting. It is being grabbed and rammed into the hot-boxes of the business mechanism. It is a dangerous makeshift. Temporarily it may seem to quiet the squeaks and chatter, but no grease-gun ever cured a machine of its fundamental flaws of design.

(c) Sooner or later this country may be catapulted
into a veritable instalment boom. More than once
Americans have been whirled into booms of the stock
market, commodities, or real estate. If so, we are
scheduled for real agonies unless we now take preven-
tive steps to educate the public so it will fight against
this potential mania.

One more thing: My literary associates object to the
title of this book. They say that people do not "buy"
on instalments, but rather "pay" on instalments.
Hence my English is poor. I agree that perhaps the
correct title would be: "The Folly of Instalment
Payment." Certainly the addicts to instalment dope,
however, begin with their *buying*.

No step in consumer protection is more urgent than
a fearless and realistic discussion of Instalment Buying. The habit of pay-as-you-go and buy-for-cash
should lead to handsome pecuniary savings. That is
the smallest of the benefits. The real gain is one of
character. The way to assure fuller and more enduring periods of prosperity is to pull people out of their
newly acquired instalmentality. Restore our early
American bargainmentality.

Although this book is directed to consumers, I am
writing it as the lifelong and loyal friend of manufacturers and retailers. With these groups my major
professional and business interests are most closely
allied. I feel that the further use of instalment "dope"
must be checked by a rebirth of common sense among
consumers. Unless that is done, industry and merchandising may suffer severely. This would mean an-

other jolt for investors, many of whom are among my clients. I therefore seek especially the coöperation of trade associations and other business organizations. I urge them, as a measure for their own self-protection —yes, self-*preservation*—to aid in the distribution of this book.

It is a pleasure to thank members of my editorial staff for their research work in this field; and in particular to acknowledge the coöperation of Martha O. Burgess, John S. Caproni, Herbert D. Downward, Charles M. Evans, E. Lafayette Quirin, John D. Riordan, Henry H. Stafford, and especially Clarence N. Stone. Acknowledgment is also given to Mr. C. R. Stiles, F.R.G.S.

R. W. B.

Babson Park, Massachusetts
April, 1938

CONTENTS

CHAPTER ONE

WHO BUYS ON INSTALMENTS AND WHY

"What you will have, quoth God, pay for it and
take it."—*Anonymous*

Paying for purchases by instalments has become an accepted and natural idea. So much so that this little story may bring the point home. One of my employees was at the barber's. Conversation led to the question as to where my employee was working. This being several miles away from home, the barber asked how he traveled to and fro. My employee said, "I take the train and it's very convenient."

"How much does it cost?"

"I buy a monthly commutation ticket and it doesn't cost much that way."

"What do you mean—you have to pay for a whole month?"

"Yes, I buy enough tickets for a whole month."

"Do you have to pay cash for a whole month's rides ahead of time?"

Evidently some people have so little cash in their pockets that even buying train tickets on the instalment plan seems likely. How can the instalment plan have become so natural as to lead the barber to make those remarks? It is because there are many different

1

branches of our business structure which boost the idea. It is because the advertising fraternity has made the accepted commonplace of today an idea which only a few years ago was in disrepute.

It is unnecessary to display the various types of instalment advertisements in this book. The help which this book can give you rests in demonstrating concealed factors. The consumer did not ask for the instalment plan. Bear that in mind. As a rule, the average customer is very apathetic. He accepts business methods as they are. The merchant, however, must make his sales. It is literally a fight among merchants for the consumer's dollar. More than that, it is a fight for the greatest share of the consumer's income.

PLIGHT OF THE "BACKWARD"

A recent instance of this battle, and the strategy behind the scenes, was released in an article entitled "Suggests Instalment Sales To Aid Textile Consumption." It reads as follows:

"Suggestions of new ways to restore stability to the fabric market are being heard on all sides at the present time. The question being most frequently asked is, 'How can fabric manufacturers get more of the consumer's dollar?' Realizing that today they must compete with the manufacturers of automobiles, radios, vacuum cleaners, electric refrigerators and countless other articles now regarded as necessities by the average householder, some in the silk industry are wondering if the aggressive, instalment sales methods of the newer industries might not be adapted to aid the textile industry.

"...Now the retailer, as illustrated by the ordinary department store, has little incentive to push the sales of garments, it is stated. What the retailer seeks is profits on sales, and it is of little moment to him whether he sells mechanical household equipment or textiles. In fact, statistics for department-store sales show that net returns on the fabric and garment departments are generally unsatisfactory.

"...'Why then do the textile industries make such a poor showing in their bid for the consumer's dollar?' asked one representative of the textile trade. Simply because as yet nobody has devised a selling method by means of which a salesman can enter our homes and sell us say $100 or $150 worth of garments on the instalment plan, that is, on a competitive basis with automobiles, radio and household appliances.... The point is that until someone does discover an aggressive and successful sales method which can enter the home the textile industry must be reconciled to take a relatively smaller and smaller portion of the consumer's income. This definitely is not a happy outlook for industries which are so important to the welfare and convenience of the ultimate consumer."

"MORE FOR US" MEANS LESS FOR YOU

The above report was of distinct interest to all merchants of textile goods. Certainly it is definite proof that instalment ideas originate merely from the desire to get more of *your* dollar. Notice that one of the main reasons for pushing the instalment plan in textiles rests on the fact that textile departments of stores are not particularly profitable; while other departments, which do sell on the instalment plan, are definitely much more profitable. Just what does that mean to the consumer? In consumer language, it means just this: The consumer gets more for his money in textiles sold on a cash basis than he does in the other lines sold on the instalment plan.

Ford Motor Company interests became concerned with the instalment selling of cars only after seeming hesitation. Apparently at one time it was their aim to meet instalment competition by inducing people to save for the purchase of a car. Advertising of automobiles, however, had been so effective that many consumers desired immediate possession. The Ford interests, presumably to sustain sales position in the industry, seem to have felt impelled to countenance the instalment-plan policy. I mention this point not because that organization was the only industrialist to face this problem with apparent reluctance; but because many will recall the Ford efforts to induce savings.

What is the result? Practically every line of business wants you to buy on the instalment plan if you cannot buy otherwise. Why? Because all are too well aware of the power of advertising. They know that if you do not bite on their particular line, advertising will make you bite on some other line of goods. Your funds will thus be depleted and then any hope of selling to you is lost.

LOW MONEY RATES A HELP—TO WHOM?

Who wants you to buy on the instalment plan? Practically everybody who cares less for you than for your dollar. That tendency is particularly marked in certain stages of the business cycle because of extremely low money rates for commercial purposes. In such periods, large finance companies can borrow money at a very low rate of interest. They turn that money over to merchants, supervise the collection of instalment payments, either directly from the consumer or by aiding the merchant, and may make as much as 1000% over the cost of the money to them!

Merchants, moreover, discovered in the instalment plan a means of making more money on a time sale than they would make on a cash basis. This is the most insidious development which has come upon us. Let us take the case of a large mail-order company where the method of instalment selling is upright. The prices marked are cash prices, and the total additional instalment charge is definitely posted. Thus the consumer, if he merely opens his eyes, can see what it costs to satisfy his desire immediately rather than later.

Consider a $49.50 radio. That is the cash price. The net profit on this sale, after overhead and sales expense, is probably $5. Of course, the gross profit is very much more; but we are concerned here with the final amount available for dividends, which in this case is probably $5. An instalment-plan sale adds $5 to the price, making the profit nearer $10. In other words, the funds of the mail-order company are so great that it can easily finance its own instalment sales. You see immediately that by tacking on an extra ?5, the net profit on that radio is increased also. Some of the additional $5 obtained from the consumer is required for increased costs due to accounting methods, additional cost of handling the payments and insuring against losses. It is only natural, under such circumstances, for most merchants to push instalment selling as much as possible. Let me take another example.

INTEREST AT 50% PER ANNUM

A clothing firm advertises suits in the $20 class, for $2 down and weekly payments at $2 each on this "convenient" plan. The additional charge for the instalment method is only $1. It looks like, and is, 5% on the amount of the sale. It, however, actually is close to a 50% interest rate, on an annual basis, for the money involved. Thus $20 being paid in the course of ten weeks makes an average outlay financed of $10 for the ten-week period, more in the first few weeks and less in the last weeks. There are five ten-week periods in a year. For example, on a sale every ten weeks, an average outlay of $10 throughout the year brings $5 additional income to the merchant! Thus 50% interest per annum! Of course, in this case collection expenses are a large proportion. Yet the consumer also has additional weekly payment expenses in time, carfare, postage and so forth! However, it is absolutely necessary in this day and age for such clothing firms to offer the instalment plan; otherwise other merchants will drain the consumer's pocketbook by that method. Even a $20 suit is placed on the instalment basis in order not to lose any sales.

High finance as a rule has shunned the instalment plan. Until recently, it has been very much as in the days when the banking system was invented. The best citizens of the community then looked upon banking as a very disgraceful proposition. In the course of time, however, the idea was so nicely developed that the best citizens of the community were bankers. Will it be the same today? Will those who have another scheme for usury be successful in climbing to the top of the social world? The answer can hardly be anything but "yes" as long as the consumer foolishly allows the seller or financier to tell him how to spend.

THE LAST FRONTIER IS REACHED

Buying on the instalment plan is little more than paying for being misled into believing it proper to consume now what one has not yet earned. All kinds of sentiment, as well as practical reasons, are placed before you to get more of your dollar. The medical profession today is toying with instalment-plan ideas. Naturally it has been feeling the effects of the consumer's empty pocketbook. Perhaps I should say, the consumer's chained payroll. The situation is such that many sincere, well-meaning doctors, week after week, have to see the earnings of their patients drained away while the bill for last year's baby is still unpaid. Competition in the business world and gullibility of the average consumer have left no place for common sense. Hence the doctors feel that they too must somehow organize an instalment-plan method to chain the patient's pocketbook, or they will simply be left holding the bag in the next depression as they were in the last. So even the community doctor today is forced to want you to pay him on the instalment plan.

PROGRESS OVERWHELMS CHARACTER

Unfortunately, the wily inducements are not always from outside. At home, the consumer faces a temptation much more difficult to resist. It is not only the desire to keep up with the Joneses. It is a growing social thought, making many people believe that they deserve more than they are at present able to buy. Every day's newspaper contains items appealingly placed before us, and repeatedly so. Take for instance a new washing machine—or rather, I must not make the mistake of calling it a washing machine. It is a complete automatic laundry.

Like television, this automatic laundry in itself is a picture of the 20th Century. All you do is put your washing in the laundry cabinet, add the soap and bluing, touch a button, and thirty minutes later, take out the wash without having to touch it in the meantime. This machine washes, rinses three times in three different waters and spins the clothes dry ready to be put on the line! Now tell me, how many housewives can resist that temptation? But the cost is $169.50.

Any statistician knows that, with so many other items clamoring for the wage-earner's dollar, it is beyond hope to expect the average consumer to buy this marvel for cash. Consumers simply do not have the money to buy it. Yet, is it not natural that many wives will plead with their husbands for the new automatic laundry? The worst part of it all is that most well-meaning husbands will actually be intrigued by the machine and feel ridiculous in resisting this new instalment-plan temptation.

Who wants you to buy on the instalment plan? Here we come to the plain facts of the matter. You yourself succumb to the temptation of the age. Why are you likely to succumb? Only for this reason: Because you do not use the arithmetic that you were taught in grammar school. Once having bought the item, will you not have to save enough money to cover the full cash price plus the charges? Then why not beat the game? Save first. Buy for cash, getting a good discount. You would thus avoid the instalment surcharge and have some money left to buy more of the things so appealingly placed before you.

The average consumer is too lazy to use his own wits in figuring that out. He does not have the guts to stand on his own feet and get more for his money. Oh yes, you will probably say that is easy advice for the wealthy but hard on the other groups. Well, do not be mistaken about it. There are still many wage earners and salaried workers who *do* use their arithmetic. They beat the game by refusing to pay dearly to have something a few months earlier than they might be able to get it for cash. Such shrewd people probably increase the buying power of those dollars by

20% throughout their lifetimes, *simply for having delayed a purchase only once in their lives!* That sounds incredible, but let me explain:

GIVING YOURSELF A LIFE SENTENCE

Notice this! *I say they postpone buying only once, save instead, and forever after get more for their money.* Why do I say that they had to postpone *only once?* Well, that is simple enough. Here is the reason.

Once the average wage-worker is loaded with instalment debt, he thereafter has to save to meet the payments. He cannot start buying anything else on the instalment plan until he has finished paying up. During that payment period, he cannot save actual cash. So, when he finally has paid up, being still without cash savings, his next purchase is likely to be again on the instalment plan. So on throughout his life. But the wise person saves cash before his first purchase. He then buys for cash, and can again save for his next purchase while the fool is only meeting the instalment payments.

When you buy on the instalment plan, the chances are that you finish the payments just at the time a new and perfected model comes on the market. What is the result? You have paid well over and above the cash price for an item that is going to be out of date when you really begin to own it. The cash buyer, who waits perhaps a year, not only pays less, but gets a better product. This is particularly so in the wide field of instalment-plan items where improvements are taking place continuously. Your impatience makes you buy on the instalment plan. It chains payments and charges around your salary because you will not wait one short year to start clean and continue clean forever after!

The instalment idea is "advertised" from the top down. The consumer sees the billboards but he does not see the source. It is interesting to note a talk which was delivered before the American Management Association. Certainly before such an august audience it takes an enlightened attitude to install confidence in this new debt machine. In that talk, experts in management of business were assured that:

"Whatever adverse economic and social effects may be chargeable to the instalment device are, in my opinion, related to the amount of the instalment debt outstanding at any given time."

The speaker proceeded to show how the amount of instalment debt outstanding at any time is only a small fraction of the total business turnover in the country. He continued:

"The instalment device, operating within limits which we have not yet begun to approach, seems to be an ideal mechanism to implement purchasing power, to stimulate production and to increase the national income to the end that we may come nearer to 'the abundant life' without doing violence to the price levels and so destroying the effective purchasing power of great numbers of people who live on fixed incomes."

The author of that long sentence is none other than an official of one of the largest finance corporations in the United States. It is deplorable that statements like those should be uttered before such an important audience. How can the purchasing power of the wage earner be increased by charging him more for what he buys?

I shall show in the chapter dealing with the possibility of another severe depression (Chapter III) that the instalment plan does not permanently increase production. Therefore, whatever stimulation it provides is merely one of the time element. It makes people buy now an article for which they otherwise would have to wait. Instalment-plan advocates fail to mention that buyers on instalment, if they continue under that system, pay instalment charges for the rest of their lives. These advocates fail to mention the penalty for having bought such instalment items, let us say, one year sooner than for cash.

Certainly this debt charge for a whole lifetime reduces the purchasing power of the wage earner. It is like a pay cut. It is at the source of many of our industrial difficulties today. The worker, being fooled, does not realize that the instalment plan is the cheat within the pay envelope. It is high time that the public be made aware of the source of such insidious ideas.

In a carefree moment, one who operates a personal loan business is rumored to have remarked: "Once they step inside my office door, I have them for life. We have the charges figured so that they cannot possibly meet them. Especially is this so when the suckers come for money to pay an instalment. For the average person, it is an absolute impossibility to earn enough to pay us what we get and the instalment companies too. They stay with us until bled dry." No wonder some people speak enthusiastically of the instalment plan!

When one secures a "personal loan" to pay an instalment, usually he is trying to pay at the rate of 50% a year on the money he doubly borrows. Economists and statisticians have figured out that the world probably can stand 2% compound interest payments because of the natural growth of production. Imagine the poor fellow who tries to buck the world with a 50% load on his meager earnings.

Even when reporting to its own stockholders, a finance company sometimes continues to follow the custom in the small loan field and refers to a rate of, say, 2½% a month. Whatever the arithmetic, psychologically that seems to sound more suitable than 30% a year.

In gas or electrical appliances, not only the merchant, but also the utility companies want you to hurry your purchase. They will be earning money on the gas or electricity you consume so much the sooner. Convenient payment plans are therefore advertised by these very influential industries. They go so far as to capitalize your debt on the basis that it will bring so much revenue to them.

PUT THE APPEAL IN REVERSE AND DODGE THE
ARITHMETIC

Obviously, the instalment plan is advertised by making you think of the item involved and by making you forget the cost: "You can buy this car at $7.45 weekly, including all charges. Your old car probably covers the down payment." There is no mention whatsoever in this advertisement of the number of weeks you will have to pay $7.45. The appeal is not that the car is a good value at the total price it will eventually cost you. The appeal is reversed to the effect that $7.45 weekly for a while is so little for the wonderful brand-new model. Of course, financiers and merchants use their arithmetic. They have found it probably *the one secret* of success above all others. Do not be surprised therefore if in trying to get the most of your dollar, they avoid making *you* think of arithmetic.

There is a little insinuation in the term "including all charges." It practically means: "Don't bother about the charges—they are all included." You may not be aware that it means an especially fat profit, not only on the instalment-financing angle, but also a nice profit on the insurance feature involved in the sale of the car.

Or perhaps the advertisement may not say "including all charges." In that case, beware even more. In fact, if you are not careful, it may mean this, which you will learn only after you have signed the contract: *Namely, the financing and insurance charges are addi-*

tional. Your weekly bill may be as much as 25% more than you thought. Oh yes, in fine print on the contract, there are probably words to the effect that these charges are additional. But a smart salesman keeps you too busy to read such "minor" details.

FISHING THE POOREST SUCKERS WITH GANG HOOKS

On the radio, for instance, you have perhaps heard how easily you can settle your debts through some financing plan. Of course, today, when there are so many people chained through repeated instalment purchases, it is only natural to find a new business pyramiding a new type of debt on top of it all. Solicitors for such debt-paying schemes would perhaps be more to the point if they said, "You bit on that hook; now in trying to wiggle off of it, here is another hook to catch you by the tail." Certainly you cannot imagine some altruistic finance company taking care of your debts without getting something also for themselves.

Did you ever think that in using the instalment plan to get "out of debt" you may actually get into a heavier debt? You may sign a contract with a creditor who may be far more heartless than the original creditor. If you cannot pay the debts you already owe, is it wisdom to sign another debt with a new creditor? Rather than that, by all means have the courage to face the creditors, show self-respect, and, if necessary, compromise with them to the fullest extent of ability to pay. Who wants you to get out of debt by getting into debt even more? Perhaps YOU do. Perhaps you want somebody to take the whip-hand of the law to force you to honor your own name.

BEWARE OF THE INFLATION ARGUMENT

Recently, there is a new type of instalment-plan booster. Let me call them the inflationists. They say that you should buy on the instalment plan because prices are going up. They claim that with inflation you would be able to pay that debt with cheap dollars. Inflation means, of course, that the supply of dollars increases and it becomes easier to pay any pre-established amount. Mark my word! Those who favor that idea have not studied inflation in foreign countries.

Who makes money in the course of inflation? The evidence is clear. It is *not* the man who is in debt and without cash. On the contrary, it is the man who has plenty of cash and who can buy, for cash, goods that will have a permanent value. The people who get into debt soon find themselves dispossessed, because there is bound to come a time in the course of inflation when many individuals will be short of cash. It is then that creditors dispossess. Consequently, those things bought on instalments, as a protection against inflation, are likely to be lost entirely.

When inflation takes place, even though there is plenty of so-called money, people will actually feel poor because prices will have gone up so much more. People who buy on the instalment plan will then actually have a harder time paying their instalments than in ordinary stable periods. The higher cost of everyday needs will leave nothing to meet instalments. If somebody wants you to buy on the instalment plan on the basis that you will be better off to take advantage of inflation, do not be misled.

As a general rule, take this for granted: People want you to buy on the instalment plan because it is so highly profitable to *them*. To you that should mean that you are giving yourself a pay cut around 10% on such purchases, and perhaps for life.

CHAPTER TWO

HISTORY OF INSTALMENT BUYING

"He who keeps out of debt grows rich."—Rabelais

In our pride of what we consider modern methods, we forget that there were "New Deals" in China, Egypt, Greece and Rome long before the Christian Age. It might be well for us to remember that the great grain, metal and slave markets of Alexandria and of Rome were just as susceptible to rumors as is our own stock market. For instance, if the Governor of a Western Province made an indiscreet remark, the commodity and equity markets in Rome reacted.

Similarly, there is nothing essentially new in instalment buying and selling. Records exist of instalment transactions which took place in Mesopotamia long before the rise of Rome. The terms of such transactions were precise and definite as to down payments and subsequent instalment payments. Turning to an era with which we are all more familiar, we find that Marcus Licinius Crassus, who lived in Rome from 105 to 53 B.C., was the great go-getter of his day. He was, as you will remember, the associate of Cæsar and Pompey in the first triumvirate. He seems to have been something of a profiteer. When land values tumbled he made real-estate investments which one historian sets at eight thousand talents, approximately ten million dollars. By placards the Roman citizenry were told that they could buy new and modern homes on suitable pieces of property without paying for them "in full" right at the beginning. They were told that arrangements could be made to pay a certain amount as an original outlay, with subsequent amounts to be paid regularly over a period of time.

One writer remarks that it is safe to believe that Crassus did well, from a profit standpoint, in his part-payment ventures. In days of relief rolls and benefit payments, it is interesting to learn that Crassus gave a feast to the people of Rome which required ten thousand tables. He even distributed to every citizen a three months' provision of corn!

CUSTOMS IN MODERN TIMES

As to more modern times, we find it stated that instalment selling was prevalent in France before the Revolution. Furniture was apparently sold on the instalment plan in England during the 18th Century. We know that here in this country, as early as 1817, a well-known furniture shop, Cowperthwait & Sons, advertised their product: "For sale on the most reasonable and accommodating terms." The first large-scale instalment selling appears to have been practiced by the Singer Company shortly after Howe patented the lock-stitch in the year 1846. The practice gradually spread to other merchandising lines such as books (in sets), pianos and organs.

The piano industry as early as 1875 developed instalment plans in a big way. Those were the days when little Mary and Johnny had to practice their piano pieces regularly even although the children were not musically inclined. The piano industry then sold the American people the idea that a piano in itself constituted a hallmark of gentility and refinement. Incidentally, with the development of the new miniature pianos of good tone and volume, we find the piano industry again staging a revival, largely through the instalment-selling route.

Instalment plans were given a great impetus during the World War when Uncle Sam himself sold Liberty Bonds on the instalment plan. I feel that these Liberty Bond campaigns did two things. For one thing, they made the general public securities conscious. The 1929 era, when the public was in the market all over, was a natural sequel. Another thing those campaigns did was to fasten the habit of instalment purchase on a great many people.

It was after the World War that instalment plans reached their full flower as the automobile industry branched out in that field. Then the last traces of social stigma, which to an extent had previously been attached to the instalment method of buying, disappeared. The practice became respectable. It is said that instalment-plan selling has enabled the automobile industry to produce cars in far greater volume. Hence, it is argued, you and I can make purchases on a much lower price basis than would hold true if such volume production had not come about. I, however, question whether this statement is true over a long term of years on a complete economic cycle. Certainly, it does not follow that the purchase of an article on the instalment plan is either the best or the cheapest proposition for individual consumers. The freight has to be paid in the form of interest charges which turn out to be higher than might at first be supposed. Hence, in the end, the volume of production may be cut down by instalment plans.

TERMS OF CREDIT CHANGE

We are now however discussing simply the history of this instalment-plan selling. In the decade between 1920 and 1930 instalment plans first became really popular. Washing machines, vacuum cleaners, electrical and gas appliances, radios, mechanical refrigerators, jewelry, musical instruments, and even securities were purchased on the basis of one's making a down payment and then a series of subsequent payments over a period of time. The mail-order and farm-implement houses adopted the practice. More and more department and clothing stores went over to the scheme. The flood mounted until in 1929 instalment sales reached a peak figure of around six and a half billions for that year. It became a common and accepted way of purchasing practically anything and everything. It is estimated that Americans buy over 60% of their new automobiles and 75% of their furniture and electrical appliances (including refrigerators, musical instruments, and radios) on time payments. In the farm-machinery field the figure probably reaches 40%; while in the jewelry field, the figure is probably as high as 25%.

Fortunately, finance companies and merchandisers periodically realize the necessity of tightening terms. Larger down payments are required and terms to maturity are shortened. Certain retail associations have advocated a two-year maximum. In the automobile field the large credit companies demand a 25% to a 33⅓% down payment in the case of new cars or fairly late models. The general term for such instalment paper has been from eighteen to twenty-four months.

FORMS OF CREDIT INFLATION

It is folly to deny that the high level of instalment sales contributes to the seriousness of a business depression. Merely to point out that the loss on instalment sales is held down to a relatively small percentage begs the point. The fact remains that the magnitude of instalment-plan sales represents a very definite degree of consumer credit inflation. It constitutes a direct contribution to the entire debt load under which we enter a depression. To say that repossessions were held down to minimum figures does not get around the fact that instalment contracts have to be completed. Just so long as a large part of the potential buying public devotes itself to whittling down old debts, then new purchasing, which would have pulled us out of the depression, is held up. In this business of instalment buying and selling, we cannot, after all, have our cake and eat it too.

I purposely confine this book to comments on conditions in the United States and in Great Britain. It is to be noted, however, that the instalment system has developed on a wide scale abroad. We find it firmly implanted in France, Germany, Sweden, Japan, Brazil, Peru, Chile and elsewhere.

Let us return now to the part which instalment plans play in our own. domestic economy. Because a great enterprise like the Singer Company has for so many years operated on the instalment-plan basis, does not mean that the situation is not serious. Some writers point out that in relation to national income, for instance, instalment-plan sales remain relatively low. To me, however, the significant thing is the increase in *tempo* of such sales within the consumer credit field. We should not shut our eyes to the fact that, in the credit field itself, more and more people are constantly asking for instalment credit.

BEWARE OF THE TEMPO

I cannot unduly stress this matter of increased tempo in instalment-plan selling because it is so closely related to the subject of this chapter. The important fact is not that a survey by the National Retail Dry Goods Association showed that the instalment sales of soft goods represent only 5.44% of total sales. The important fact is that such instalment sales were 46.39% higher than the year before! Almost anything, from neckties to automobiles, can be purchased on instalments. An estimate by the Bureau of Foreign and Domestic Commerce shows that of the total credit granted by retail establishments in a normal year (estimated at over twelve and a half billions of dollars) 36% is extended on the instalment basis. Remember that these figures are not estimates of *total* consumer credit, but that they relate only to such credit extended by *retailers*.

What concerns me is the *rate of increase* at which this instalment-plan habit may be fastening itself on the average consumer. A sampling test covering 1,920 credit-granting stores, shows that cash sales for 1936 increased 11.2%, while open credit sales increased 14.5% for the same year. *Instalment sales, however, increased 25.4%* that year. There is significance in these figures in relation to the factor which I have described as the increasing *tempo* of instalment buying. This is the serious fact which a study of the history of instalment buying shows.

Outside of the retail credit field itself, one should give thought to such items as personal finance company loans and funds loaned by credit unions; as well as those which are obtained through the personal loan departments of industrial banks, building and loan associations, and other such agencies. Before one contends that this matter of credit extended to instalment buyers is nothing serious, he should look at the picture in its entirety. One should take into account where we may be going, in relation to this whole business, as well as where we now are.

OFFICIAL COGNIZANCE

In the history of instalment plans, we reached the point in 1938 where the Government itself, through

the Department of Commerce, took official cognizance
of the situation. The Department is to be applauded
for this interest which it is taking in a decidedly important economic problem. An Instalment Credit
Unit has been set up at Washington under the direction of the Bureau of Foreign and Domestic Commerce. The aim is to meet a growing demand for
specific information on instalment credit. An effort
will be made to cover such items as the nature and
type of goods sold, selling terms and geographical differentials in the extension of instalment credit. It is
hoped that eventually it will be possible to set up a
current index which will definitely indicate from
month to month, or perhaps from quarter to quarter,
the precise position of instalment credit. When that
has been achieved, we shall have got somewhere.
So let us give the Department of Commerce all the
help that we can by putting no impediments in its way.

It is not to be expected that such a startling development as the growth of instalment plans could come
about without the eventual necessity for regulation and
control. I say this, frankly admitting that Government regulation has in many instances been much
overdone and has become very burdensome. Misgivings as to human fallibility, however, constitute no
reason why we should let this instalment credit situation develop into a Frankenstein sequel wherein we
may all be destroyed.

The *volume* of consumer credit now extended by
retailers may not be so great. Hence, we may not
need to feel that the *volume* of such business now is

unduly alarming. *But what about the tempo?* These views have been expressed in a speech made by Mr. Wilford L. White, Chief of Marketing Research Division, Bureau of Foreign and Domestic Commerce, in a talk given before the Conference on Consumer Financing, held at the University of Chicago. What impressed me particularly was Mr. White's direct statement, *"The rate of* INCREASE *of instalment sales, however, is so much greater than for cash and open-credit sales* that this method of extending credit to consumers should closely be watched." With Mr. White's statement I most whole-heartedly agree!

RISE OF FINANCE COMPANIES

It was natural that as the practice of instalment selling spread in this country, large financing companies arose to furnish the "implementing." As early as 1908, finance companies had started on a small scale. Commercial Credit Company was incorporated in 1912. In 1915, John N. Willys formed a finance company with the direct purpose of stimulating automobile sales on an instalment basis. That company was taken over by Commercial Credit in 1922. In the meanwhile, in 1919, General Motors Acceptance Corporation had been started. Commercial Investment Trust had been organized in 1915. Universal Credit Corporation, originally formed in 1928, was taken over by Commercial Investment Trust in 1933, although it continues to be operated under its own identity as a separate division. In addition to the Big Three, we find more than 500 local finance companies with offices spread throughout the United States. The latter usually have no direct tie-up with producers. They are able to compete with the Big Three because they are willing to accept non-recourse paper which does not necessarily bear the direct endorsement of the dealer making the sale.

An event which forms a direct part of the history of instalment plans was the attempt in 1937 of the Department of Justice to prosecute three major automobile companies and associated finance firms. This was for company practices which, it was alleged, were violations of the Anti-Trust Law. The Attorney General refused to agree to Consent Decrees. The Department of Justice continued the presentation of its case to a Federal grand jury at Milwaukee. Claims were made of "dealer-coercion." The Court, however, dismissed the case over a "question of propriety." Government counsel insisted that further action would be instituted in some other Federal judicial district. It was subsequently intimated that the investigation of automobile financing practices had been initiated upon complaints by independent finance companies.

It is interesting to note that there has been in committee in Congress a resolution appropriating $50,000 for an investigation of relations between the automobile manufacturing companies and their dealers. It is proposed that such investigation be made under the auspices of the Federal Trade Commission. The aim would be to try to determine whether or not manufacturers are responsible for unfair competition and low profits among dealers. On the other side, it has been contended that the net result of any restrictions which may be imposed upon the automobile companies might increase the price of automobiles to consumers. Surely Washington squalls are ahead for certain branches of the instalment industry. A news commentator of national prominence asserts, "Abuses there are no doubt in this field, but, like other questions of unfair competition and fair trade practice, they are subjects either for Federal Trade Commission inquiry or for civil suits."

FEDERAL RESERVE INCREASES THE DANGER

Another milestone in the history of instalment selling was reached in 1937. I refer to the action which the Federal Reserve Board took in relation to liberalizing the eligible list of commercial paper. The Board's regulations were broadened so as to include paper drawn to finance instalment sales of a commercial character. It is true that the Board very wisely stipulated that such eligible instalment paper must have a maturity, at time of discount, of not more than ninety days. *However, who is to say that a future Board may not at some time extend the period?* In fact, an exception was soon made in the case of agricultural paper concerns when a maturity of not more than nine months was ruled acceptable.

It was at first supposed that the broadening of these Federal Reserve Board regulations applied only to the paper of concerns specifically engaged in the instalment credit business. It was subsequently stated, however, that private commercial instalment paper, which had been accepted by banks, would be eligible for discount when meeting the other regulations. Instalment paper, which had hitherto been looked at askance in banking circles, has now been legitimatized. The Board was very specific in ruling that a member bank may accept the note of a "householder who uses the proceeds to purchase household equipment such as radio and furniture," with assurance that such a note will be discountable if meeting the ninety-day maturity requirement. It must be remembered that the Federal Reserve Board restricts discounting to notes "arising out of actual commercial transactions." In its clarifying statement, however, the Board gave this restriction an exceedingly liberal interpretation. It took the position that a consumer's note "is to finance the final step in the distribution of goods."

INSTALMENT SALES CREATE CHATTEL MORTGAGES

Many people overlook, when discussing this whole subject, that an instalment sale represents essentially a transaction which involves what is virtually a chattel mortgage. Sometimes the instalment note itself contains a provision of that nature and sometimes repossessions are effected by securing, through court procedure, what is known as a deficiency judgment. Instalment purchases surely represent a process of going into debt. The extent to which instalment selling has been practiced in this country does not tell us the story of what will happen in the future. When more and more individual consumers have been urged to place debts of varying maturities on their backs, the

result can be very serious. Because this direct extension of banking into the mercantile field did not involve the United States in serious trouble during 1929-
1935, is no proof that trouble may not be ahead of us.
Impartial economists agree that the burden of instalment debt played some part in that depression. The
advocates of instalment sales tell us that the "potentialities" of such business have scarcely been ex-
plored! Surely when the next depression comes instalment selling will meet its real test. Let us hope
that it will not be its Waterloo or that of the country
in general!

Among the "potentialities," about which we hear so
much, is included the extension of instalment selling
to so-called soft goods, such as clothing, minor household furnishings, linen, glassware, etc. The extension
of instalment selling into the soft-goods line is certainly something that will bear careful watching.

That an individual of comparatively small means
can get himself into serious trouble on this score is
definitely indicated by an item of recent legislation.
Ordinarily, of course, such an individual would run
the risk of having his wages garnisheed, i.e., attached.
The State of Wisconsin has passed a law, however,
providing that a debtor who earns less than $2400 a
year may, by suitable court action, obtain the appoint-
ment of a trustee. That trustee could, in turn, be
empowered to negotiate a scaling down of debts over
a two-year period. During that time, in relation to
such debts, the individual debtor himself would be
garnishee-free. There is some reason to believe that

in the course of time this law will be copied by other states. Whither are we going?

WHAT OF THE FUTURE?

We perhaps have not had a long enough historical period in respect to instalment plans to enable us to draw the conclusions at which some writers have so easily arrived. Granted that there were no undue losses in this field during past depressions, who is to say that the future will tell a similar tale? It seems quite probable that when the country enters the next depression instalment sales will have reached a figure much larger than anything previously seen. Then will come the real test. It simply cannot be denied that instalment selling in itself is definitely one form of inflation. Unless we can control this evil the effect in the future will be something quite different from what it has been in the past. You cannot have The Average Citizen stagger into a depression under a heavy burden of individual debt without something serious happening. Losses will have to be taken. By whom?

Unfortunately, a good part of the literature obtainable with respect to this whole problem comes from those who are profiting from instalment selling. It is a little beside the point to argue that instalment credit still remains only a small portion of total consumer credit. For one thing, even a relatively small percentage figure can sometimes be of great importance. We all know, for instance, that the percentage of our export of foreign trade, in relation to general business, is very small as compared with the amount of our domestic trade. Nevertheless, it is this smaller foreign trade figure which in itself very often spells the difference between good and bad general business. Furthermore, will the figure for instalment sales remain small in proportion to total consumer credit?

I might feel somewhat differently about instalment selling if I could see some way in which it might be controlled. If it would be used simply as a stimulant when employment is below normal and then discontinued gradually as general business rises above normal, it might perform a useful function. The trouble is, however, that instalment selling seems to be proving to be something like a drug which must again and again be resorted to, once it has been used. We, therefore, should ask what the final results may be on the great consuming public.

As the so-called potentialities of instalment plans are pushed more and more to an extreme, what will be the result upon our nation? We may find our nation eventually in the same state that one would find a physical body which had again and again been shot full of some powerful stimulant. We all know that, in the latter case, a point would be reached where a complete collapse would ensue. Certainly, the business and wages activity created by instalment-plan selling does not put into the hands of consumers the amount of money which will enable them to get out from under the debt burden which they have assumed. The effect is like spinning the rear wheels of an automobile stuck in the mud—the more you spin the deeper you get.

CHAPTER THREE

INSTALMENTS AND THE BUSINESS CYCLE

"He that goes aborrowing goes asorrowing."—*Franklin*

Bill Pep is in the furniture business, and is a very successful merchant at that. He started in the business from the bottom and worked through the years, always full of new ideas, and has turned out to be one of the best merchandisers of furniture in his town. Of course, that means that he is on the lookout for all the customers that he can possibly get. He learned in the Twenties, in the midst of a big building boom, how successful the furniture business could be.

It was Bill Pep's very special insight that permitted him to sell furniture as readily as he did. You recall the Twenties, of course. The automobile was fast becoming America's great institution. Many people were building homes. Credit was being extended in all directions. Yet Bill Pep was having a difficult time finding customers with ready cash. It seemed that more and more of the newlyweds had practically no cash reserves. As for others, the cost of the new homes which the Joneses and the Smiths were building was nearly always several hundred or a thousand dollars more than they had planned to pay.

It seemed that Bill Pep would lose many customers

if he did not adopt the plan of allowing people to pay by small amounts over an extended period. In fact, he found that he had to push that plan. There was no doubt that people wanted furniture. More and more customers would flock to his store as he reduced each instalment payment to a lower figure while extending the period of payment over a longer and longer stretch.

MERRILY WE ROLL ALONG

You see, Bill Pep was in business to make a profit and to move goods. Other considerations were secondary. In fact, he was so obsessed with the urge to sell goods that it mattered little to him how he received payment. Credit could be extended to him to tide over the period when his customers were paying by instalments. In fact, as business along this line was increasing, he gained more experience.

To his pleasant surprise, the average customer was not concerned really with the cost of an item, but rather with the weekly payment. It seemed that neither Mr. Jones nor Mrs. Smith would take the trouble to figure out the total cost of their payments. They would immediately forget the total amount and consider only the small weekly instalment. This promptly opened a new avenue of profits for Bill Pep. He could boost his margin of profit without the customer's appreciating the fact. Of course this was considered quite pardonable, because after all it was still the way he could sell the most furniture. People's cash funds were low; their needs, they felt, were great. Why try to row against the tide when through clever merchandising one could increase his business and profits with the instalment plan?

There came a time, however, when the building boom was on the decline. Even though Bill was aggressive, had initiative and faith in his merchandising, this could not prevent the building boom from spiraling down—slowly at first, then with increasing speed.

It was not only in the building line that business began to slacken. The stock market crash wiped out many Joneses and Smiths whose homes were fully mortgaged. They were depending on stratosphere prices to pay the half yearly instalment on the mortgage. Moreover, by clever switching from one tip to another, they planned to pay also the instalment on the furniture. Farmers' large crops had to be sold at lower and lower prices. As the purchasing power of one section of the nation began to suffer, the effects spread to all lines.

SALVATION OR SALVAGE?

While the Smiths and Joneses might lose their new homes because it was too much of a load for them ever to hope to salvage, they saw their way clear to keep their furniture. (How many grocers and doctors know it!) The payments already made on the furniture resulted in the balance being far less than the furniture was worth. The situation for the furniture was therefore quite unlike the heavy mortgage on the house. They needed furniture anyway, while, on the other hand, they could readily move to a rented house.

This rapidly declining balance due on any one sale gives astounding security for the dealer and finance companies. This has led many business men, economists, financiers and politicians to look upon the instalment system as quite apart from the various causes of booms and depressions. They overlook, however, that an unusually long period of sharply curtailed buying would have to follow every boom of instalment sales. It is not without cause that we had an extraordinary depression in the early Thirties. Eventually we emerged from those bad times. Nevertheless, at any given time, whatever the situation, before we start humming along too merrily, let us ask ourselves, "Will there be another severe depression?"

HEARTLESS ECONOMIC LAW

Remember that economics is the study of the relationship between human nature, society and the material world. Students of history all recognize that human nature changes very slowly, although some political or business developments may proceed rapidly. Despite inherent difficulties, economics is now developing into a science. One can no longer consider himself an economist unless he is also a statistician; nor can one consider himself a statistician unless he has mastered the laws of physics and mathematics which are all-pervading.

Economics is no longer abstract philosophy. Booms and depressions are caused by hard mathematical laws, from production to distribution. One of these is the law of acceleration in the output of capital goods in relation to the production of consumer goods. Capital goods, once produced, remain as a source of further production or use, for a fairly long period of time. Consumer goods are rather quickly consumed. The relation is probably best explained, and you will readily understand it, by considering the growth of the automobile industry.

SLOWER INCREASE MEANS DECREASE

Readers recall that during the building boom of the Twenties a fairly large factor was the building of garages and expansion of factories—factories not only in which to build the automobiles, but in which to build machinery to manufacture the automobiles. Thus, as more and more automobiles were being placed on the roads, the Smiths and Joneses needed more garages. The automobile boom resulted in a tremendous increase in garage building. On the other hand, as soon as the increase in automobile registrations became a smaller amount from one year to the next, fewer new garages were needed each year. Thus a mere slowing up of the rate of advance in automobile manufacture meant an actual decrease from one year to the next in the number of garages built! Here is a mathematical relationship resting upon the dynamics of production trends.

So it is in the machine-tool industry. For the same reason, when the number of automobiles built increases by a smaller amount, so must the demand for new machinery actually decrease. You can readily understand how such a process applies to other industries.

It may be more difficult to see through this problem when it is applied to the entire business structure. Yet in this age 50% of our activity is in industries other than consumer goods like food, minimum shelter and clothing. Hence the law described above must therefore apply to our social and business organization as a whole. Even "planning," as virtuous an ideal as that may be, cannot change this hard fact. Perhaps this sad thought can be made more convincing when we think of a law which, I regret, is too infrequently pondered and is sometimes even ridiculed.

BUMPER CROPS OF WILD OATS

I speak of the law of Action and Reaction. I can perhaps best state it in this way: *Every excessive social or business movement carries along with it the seed of its own defeat.* This is particularly so, human nature being what it is. As an example, let me take you back to the Twenties again, and discuss another boom which received far more publicity than the building boom. I refer to the stock-market craze. Oh yes! We were then in a "new era." The Federal Reserve System was the planned "New Deal" of the day. With such a marvelous banking system, depressions were said to be a thing of the past! Most people thought it was foolish to expect stocks henceforth to sell as low as formerly. In that new era, stocks should sell not at ten times, but rather at twenty, even thirty times earnings, they contended. "Are not these higher figures the average which results from boom and depression earnings? Is not an average yield of 5% obtained from 10% on earnings over good years, and nothing in bad years? Since bad years are no longer to be seen, a yield of 5%, or prices at twenty times earnings, is reasonable!" This was their argument.

So "investors" (they were not called speculators or gamblers) raised stock prices to a level which to them appeared reasonable on the assumption of conditions of permanent prosperity. Now, in that particular case, the seed of defeat was in the raising of prices. The very fact that prices were being raised to such heights resulted in the defeat of prosperity, even had it been otherwise possible. Wise investors sold when prices were lifted to those heights, since there was nothing further to gain anyway. That very selling hastened the reaction. This brief outline clearly shows that individual initiative alone or planned Federal Reserve Systems, are not cures for depressions!

EVIDENCE OF THE CYCLES

I have before me a Babson chart of the Physical Volume of Business in the United States, from 1871 to the present. A mere glance at this chart gives two irrefutable conclusions: (1) prosperity is followed by depression from the earliest years on; (2) the cycles have a tendency to show greater excesses of prosperity and depths of depression as we progress from decade to decade. Why have the cycles been more accentuated as we have progressed from the early industrial stage of the Seventies to the more recent times? As society progresses into the more advanced stages of capital goods, mathematical dynamic laws cause greater periods of prosperity and depression.

That is the main reason. It is not because business judgment today is inferior to that of our grandfathers. Some might say that grandchildren have less initiative. I, too, am inclined to think so; but upon deeper thought I am impressed with the fact that this is an old, old world. It would seem quite strange for a unique decrease in initiative to overtake the world suddenly at this particular epoch. No, what appears as a lack of initiative and what might lead to that false conclusion is merely the result of a new social or business organization. The natural order of things nowadays is that there are fewer independent business men in proportion to the total working population. Business is getting bigger, and a greater percentage must remain employees.

These amplitudes in the business cycles are getting bigger and bigger because we are getting more into the business fields which do not pertain solely to food, clothing and minimum shelter. Take for instance the automobile industry. Even though automobiles are consumed by individuals, their use is somewhat akin to that of capital goods. They have a long period of use. Take the newer radio cabinets, washing machines, electric or gas refrigerators, and similar merchandise; again we find a long period of use in all these instalment-plan items.

The automobile, therefore, was but the beginning of a huge surge to greater and greater heights of activity in those types of goods which have a long life of

use. The boom of the Twenties and the depression of
the Thirties formed naturally the most accentuated
cycle of prosperity and depression that this country
ever experienced. It came at a time when the greatest
percentage of our business organization was devoted
to the capital goods industries.

QUACK! QUACK! THE DOLLARS!

To be sure, there are monetary factors. Doubtless
our banking system has many quirks. It, however,
has been a very productive invention. As a scheme for
enabling business men to get along without cash, the
banking system certainly merits an award. Banking
has been extremely successful as a fundamental productive force. That may explain why monetary factors have suffered the brunt of the blame for business
cycles.

Do not misunderstand me. I do not wish to belittle
the monetary influences. In these days, however,
when some believe that monetary cures are the sole
requirement for restoring prosperity, it is time to give
a word of warning. The day of disillusion will come.
Variations in factors of money and banking, without
a doubt, have had considerable influence in the development of prosperities and depressions. But mark
my word! In the future again, as in the late Twenties, "brain trusts" will find that no matter what new
banking machinery they have, depression will seep
through.

Analysis clearly shows that monetary factors have
been more influential in the timing of trends within the

cyclical process, rather than as the major influence. As a matter of fact, even the monetary factors are becoming *more* vicious rather than less. Take one field alone—that of government financing. So much reliance is now being placed on the income tax, which in great part is a profit tax, that Federal finances are subject to greater and greater swings. This is a secondary result of the deeper amplitudes in the business cycle.

NEW AND STEEPER ROLLER COASTERS!

These extremes in Federal finances are becoming a pyramiding process. When we run into depressions, the tendency now is to get the Government into debt, to alleviate the monetary system in the business world. Of course, the deeper the Government gets into debt, the higher we must raise income taxes. The higher we raise income taxes, the greater the fluctuations in the Government's income!

Not only that, but as income taxes are raised, margins of profit become narrower. So business men are induced to go into greater excess of business, while business is good. To reap quickly while the sun is shining, they push the instalment sales, only to suffer more severely in the ensuing depressions. If monetary factors were the cure, shall we now say that we are much wiser than we were in the Twenties? Did we not think we had a good system then? Was not the Federal Reserve System regarded as the acme of monetary organization?

This chapter is not meant to be a course in economics. The subject is too broad to discuss in a few pages. It is meant rather to bring down to earth many visionaries and carefree consumers. Especially must those visionaries who are inclined to see in money and credit the sole motivating force of our entire business structure be apprehended. Once for all, progress can come only through sheer, hard, intelligent work. Here we come to a very sly insinuation so often used in defense of the instalment plan, namely that it permits greater productivity; that it is merely a new function of the monetary system. They say more people can buy, and therefore the system creates more employment.

Now there would be some truth in that idea if the goods sold on the instalment plan were about to be produced. However, that is not so. Instalment purchases are of goods already produced. The employment and payrolls were in operation before those goods were bought by the consumer. That's the nigger in the debt pile! How different it would be were the mass of workers to order goods, and then obtain employment to produce them!

Do you see what I mean? Watch the instalment process grow and what do you see? Merchants, finding newer fields in which to reap from the seed of debt, with mortgages on future payrolls, can sell their stocks on hand and reorder. *But they cannot continue the process unless instalment debt keeps on spiraling upward.* In goods of the type that last— those subject to the dynamic laws described above— when once the acceleration slows up, related industries must suffer sharp decreases in output. Thus the instalment plan is merely accentuating the waves of prosperity and depression.

It has other elements, however, which are equally vicious in their influence on the business cycle. Let us take an historic lesson, so sharp that we did not soon get over the headache. In 1936 and 1937, a greater proportion of sales on the instalment plan were made than ever before in the history of the country. Naturally with sales so good, wages would be raised. Industry finally yielded to the clamor for higher wages. Unfortunately, wages were raised much faster than industry could reduce costs. We shall see what happened.

A CHALLENGE TO UNION LEADERSHIP

Before I proceed, allow me here a comment on the way. It seems that in many cases where wages were raised, labor efficiency actually decreased. This is a very sad commentary on human nature. The greatest need of this nation is a union leadership based wholly on the idea of its union members being top-notch, grade A, sincere, efficient workers—men who will command top wages simply because industrialists cannot afford to overlook their usefulness. That offers a money-making and glorious opportunity for a far-sighted union leader!

With that off my mind, I can continue. Naturally, as costs went up, prices had to follow, and what happened? Remember that automobiles are sold in great part on the instalment plan, with a down payment figured on the basis of the value of the car turned in. Most sales, of course, are to people who already have cars. Thus when Mr. Smith was going to turn in his old model Ford or Chevrolet for a new model, what was his great surprise? He found that a substantial cash payment was required, and considerably more than he had anticipated. Surely it seemed impossible.

Automobile prices, he had been told, had gone up only 10% to 14%. Ah yes! only 10% to 14%, but on the new car price! That meant $100 or so. He had expected to turn in his car worth $350 and face a payment, or instalment debt, of $350 more. But the trade-in value of his old car was hardly affected. So he soon learned that the balance due would be, not $350, but $450. That meant an advance of 30% above the outlay he had figured.

Thus, with so many people buying on the instalment plan, the moderate increase had a tremendous effect far beyond the apparent increase. The consumer's cash on hand was constantly being held down by the drain of prior instalment payments. The consumer had no reserve to span the jump of 30% in the outlay cost of automobiles. The average consumer's wages had been raised only in proportion to the 14% advance in prices! That's why automobile sales suddenly vanished in the latter months of 1937; while the small cash retail business suffered very little.

PROS AND CONS OF THE "CON" GAME

We have heard a great deal in recent years about confidence; and I for one believe that confidence is a great factor in the process of business cycles. Perhaps it would be well to dwell a little on this factor. Would it be possible, perhaps, to avoid future depressions if somehow business men, workers, and society in general could have confidence not only in business conditions, but also in the Government? Here perhaps it would be wise to question whether the average person knows what confidence really is.

Confidence is faith. It is at the source therefore of action or inaction. Naturally, if people have faith that they can attain their objective, they go after it more resolutely. If a business man has faith that he can make a profit, presumably he will set about doing business and employing workers as long as he remains confident. Too few, however, think of the fact that confidence is only the source of action. A chemist would call it a catalyst. A catalyst is something which speeds up chemical processes, without changing them. When confidence is at work, therefore, what happens depends upon the economic ingredients with which we start. If fundamental economic conditions are sound for revival and prosperity, confidence will certainly usher in such a wholesome period. If the economic ingredients are unsound—if the seed is that of a weed instead of a fruit—confidence will lead to disaster.

Did we not have confidence in 1929? Did not business have confidence in the Government under the Hoover Administration? You and I know that there was no lack of such confidence. The facts are quite clear. The economic ingredients were leading to de-

pression, and confidence for a time only accentuated
the evil.

Confidence is the fertilizer of business, and what
grows out of the business field depends upon what seed
is sown and the care with which the field is maintained. Thus, unfortunately, while we can look to
confidence as a source of progress where conditions are
favorable, we cannot look to it for permanent prosperity. It cannot prevent a severe depression!

HAVEN OR MIRAGE?

What of the future? Many know that hair-raising
developments are always taking place in this country.
On the one hand, we have plans for social security.
Yet, on the other hand, we find the prospect that such
plans can be defeated by the very seed sown with the
social security ideal—namely, the seed of inflation.
Inflation is debt. The reason so many do not see it is
because it is a debt *of* you and me *to* you and me,
using the government as our accountant. The idea of
social security is not exactly a new one—but do not
make the mistake of assuming consequently that we
know how to run the machinery. It is distinctly new
in practical application, so far as this nation is concerned. It is new the world over on the scale and in
the manner that it is being carried out for this generation. It carries with it many implications, but none
of them can alter the mathematical relationships of
production, prices and instalment sales. Many of the
social security features can accentuate the monetary
quirks of modern society.

There is no need to assign any one cause for the next severe depression. Not alone because of human nature, but because of the very characteristic of our industrial organization, it is certain that another severe depression is ahead of us.

I hear a voice saying, "What about Russia and her successful five-year plans? Has Russia not proved that planning can avoid depressions?" It is characteristic of idealists to live peacefully through any quagmire. Remember this, the Russian episode of starvation in 1932 and 1933 was already within the span of their five-year plans. Russia fought through it ruthlessly. However, for the Russian people (as Russia was organized) that episode of famine was certainly a depression.

Russia so far is still in the very early stages of industrialization. Consequently, its booms and depressions, regardless of planning, are likely to be minor ones characteristic of nations where the capital goods industries are in their early stages of growth. Such industries have not yet come into final fruit and made themselves felt to the full throughout the consuming masses of the nation. The effects of changes in the rate of consumption or demand so far have not been felt because they have not yet arrived. The day will come when Russia will face the complete shut-down of some of its now prosperous industries.

Those who favor economic planning, however, do have something in their favor. Doubtless planning can do much. In fact, the progress of our great industries rests upon daring and intelligent planning. I have often outlined in the press a plan (the so-called Quota Plan) for reviving business activity in this country. Such planning I hope would initiate a rather long and sound period of prosperity. Yes, I am glad to answer that question, "What about planning?" Here is my answer: "Wise are they who plan on the basis of hard economic law. Fools plan only on prosperity!"

CHAPTER FOUR

"A man in debt is so far a slave."—*Emerson*

One morning the class had been devoting its time to a discussion of economics and selling. To find out just how much the boys knew about present-day distribution, the teacher asked who could describe what was meant by instalment selling. A hand shot up into the air with great gusto! Johnnie was a member of a family which had been obliged to stretch the dollar to the limit. *He* knew more about instalment buying than many of the other members of the class. He had seen a vacuum cleaner, a radio, a set of furniture and an old second-hand car delivered to his home. "Well, Johnnie," said the teacher, "tell your version of instalment selling." "You see," said the boy, "here is how:

You go	**IN**	to buy
You	**STALL**	in paying
But you	**MEaNT**	to keep the goods."

There are two viewpoints from which to look at the instalment business: (1) from the business man's point of view; and (2) from the customer's angle. What seems good for one may be bad for the other.

But right here, let me say this: For a business to continue to be successful for any length of time, a sale must be satisfactory to both the seller and the customer. A concern may use sales methods which temporarily boost its business to boom proportions; but are the customers satisfied? Unless they are, this sky-rocketing success will be short-lived. The sign on the door, instead of saying "Enter," may read "Gone Out of Business." Remember this: Satisfied customers will keep you in business; dissatisfied customers may put you in the poorhouse.

If you are doing business on the instalment plan you must be extremely cautious, for at best it has many disadvantages. At times business comes slowly. The salesmen fail to produce as many orders as they have in the past. Something must be done, and done quickly, or there will be red ink aplenty on the balance sheet. As a result, some new scheme must be tried. If people's incomes are smaller, why not cater to their pocketbooks? Out go the ads! "So much down and so much a week," "Buy now and pay tomorrow," "Enjoy a fur coat while paying for it," etc. Instalment selling under these conditions has the same effect as a stimulant administered to a sick person. Instalment selling may revive sales but does it build up a permanent clientele? Any stimulant loses its exciting effect if carried to excess. Therefore, my warning to the business man is to look on instalment selling as he would the lighting of a match. A match can light a bonfire to keep one from freezing; but if not carefully watched, the fire may spread and cause great loss.

DEPRESSIONS SPUR INSTALMENT SELLING

During periods of business recession more and more of the ambitious firms take up this form of selling. Are they running into the cross-currents of stormy waters? The whole system of distribution is a complex one. It is like an octopus with its tentacles reaching out in all directions, and involving all phases of industry and trade.

There are the cash and carry, the cash and delivery, the open credit, the coöperative, the instalment and finance corporations and the fly-by-night outfits. The concern which adds instalment to its many other forms of selling is building a structure which may need some props when the next storm signals are hoisted. Only recently some of the large and high-grade stores have been urging customers to buy on a three-payment plan, paying one-third a month for three consecutive months, with no interest or carrying charge. They are advising the use of budget accounts for the purchase of coats and furs. There are shopping coupons which demand a small deposit, plus a small carrying charge, with the balance to be paid in five equal monthly payments. Instalment selling may be a business getter, but what are the costs and consequences?

I turn now to the vital view of instalment buying, namely, the consumer's angle. Try as one may to eliminate instalment selling from our modern life, or push it into the background of the distribution archives, this cannot be done without a vigorous struggle. Instalment selling seems to be here to stay! It has been going through a process of formation and reformation. Today it alluringly offers everything for which the customer could possibly ask. There are instances when this form of purchasing an article may be plausible economically. I am now thinking of such occasions as when one wishes to buy a home. Many people feel it is far better to be putting money (in the form of instalment payments) into the purchase of a home than to be paying rent all their lives·and owning nothing after long years of such payments. Coöperative banks have been of great help in this connection and this form of instalment buying is one of the best. This is an example of what I mean when I say that at times instalment purchasing seems to offer some economic justification. In another chapter you will find mentioned various instalment purchases which are relatively justifiable and others which are relatively vicious.

THE CONTRACT MAY BE YOUR NEMESIS

Granting that instalment buying is here to stay, every customer should know what this means to his pocketbook. First let him decide whether he wants to join the ranks of these weekly or monthly payers who are forming an ever-increasing line up the steps to Debtors' Hall. Does he want the goods enough to take the risks involved? Each individual knows his own situation better than anyone else. The purchaser is the one to decide whether an investment of this kind is justifiable. Every case should be decided on its own merits.

If you should decide to sign one of these contracts, look before you leap. Do not let any rapid-fire salesman rush you into signing on the dotted line. Look the contract over at your leisure. Make sure of the facts presented therein. It is better to go slowly than be sorry. A good reliable firm which will stand back of its products and its contracts is the only one to be considered. It is much easier to sign a contract than it is to get released from one. Ask someone who has tried it.

USES OF INSTALMENT PLANS

Here are some of the reasons set forth by those who advocate instalment selling:

1. It may encourage thrift. A person who has signed a contract to pay in instalments is forced to "save" in order to have the money when these payments come due. Many persons imagine that it is easier to pay for an article after they have possession of it than it is to try and save for it in advance. They may set a sum aside each week thinking they will spend it for a vacuum cleaner, for example. Then they change their minds and use some of the money for cash purchases of some smaller articles. There goes the good intention to save, and the vacuum cleaner is still a dream. Those who claim that instalment buying encourages thrift, believe that this habit of planning and saving to meet these payments continues with the

customer after his instalment purchase debt has been paid completely.

2. It enables a person who lacks ready cash to buy those things which make for enjoyment, ease, time saving, a few months before he otherwise would take possession. He can enjoy the use of such articles while he is paying for them. If he buys an automobile on the instalment plan perhaps he can use it sooner as a means of getting to his place of employment or in contacting customers. He saves time traveling by automobile, in many instances. This time can be put to profitable use. The automobile has become almost a necessity in our modern business world. It is a sort of "buy-as-you-go" proposition. It is one of the few articles purchasable on the instalment plan which is not severely frowned upon by those who are not in sympathy with our present extensive instalment program. In other instances, a radio, electric refrigerator, washing machine or vacuum cleaner may give a few additional hours of pleasure or save a few hours of drudgery if purchased on the instalment plan.

3. For better or for worse, instalment selling has made possible a new source of credit. It has enabled the small consumer to have the credit privileges which formerly were open only to the favored class. Many individuals and families who formerly were unable to secure open-account credit now enjoy instalment credit.

4. American industry has found the instalment plan of selling one means of quickening distribution in emergencies. For example, during the World War,

industry had been geared up to large-scale production. Afterwards it was faced with the problem of disposing of large productions. By means of instalment selling retailers were able to move goods from their shelves. Wholesalers and manufacturers were also enabled to move their goods and continue activities.

5. How has the instalment plan affected unit cost of production? If we take the automobile as an example, we find that a very large proportion of the cars bought are paid for through a finance company. Thousands of customers could never have bought a car when they did, if they had had to pay cash for it. But since the way was opened for them to become a customer, sales mounted and production was put on a mass basis. It is asserted that this resulted in reducing production costs per unit. The contention is that increased sales make lower prices *for all*. It should be remembered, however, that this increase in sales, caused by instalment-plan buyers, is only temporary, or can occur but once. Furthermore any abnormal increase is followed by an abnormal decrease when, for some other reason, general business and employment suffer.

6. The standard of living is raised for a few months before it otherwise would be. Instalment selling spreads temporarily the purchasing power of an individual over a wider range of industries than if he had to pay a large amount of cash for some product and thus could purchase only one article at a time. He can have the simultaneous use of several labor-saving machines. He can purchase a home and furnish it on

the instalment plan if he so desires. Proponents declare that instalment purchasing has helped to raise the standard of living in this country, although opponents take an opposite view. Those who profit by instalment plans describe them as a means of attaining cultural improvement and aiding industry. They call the instalment system a creator of ambition; a producer of work, wealth and enjoyment. Education is often paid for in instalments. Instalment selling puts in front of every-day Main Street customers the goods which Wall Street customers have shown them are desirable to own. The Forgotten Man is thus able to purchase goods of quality although it may cost him more than if he paid cash. If it were not for the instalment method of buying, it is argued, many customers would have to be content with poor quality goods. If so, the standard of living for the customer on Main Street has been materially raised.

7. Instalment selling temporarily has a part in the employment picture. As it grew, it increased the number of workers tremendously. It has been a primary cause of taking people from the farms to the cities. Such advances in employment and payrolls, of course, have followed through temporarily to other lines of industries. These have increased their purchasing. If we have mass production, we must have mass consumption. Mass production gives remunerative employment in direct and related industries. Continued production, at a profit, is measured by capacity for consumption. This latter item is to a large extent

proportionate to the volume of employment required to consummate production.

8. Budgeting has become a by-word in many households throughout the country. From Government budgeting the practice has spread to industrial and commercial organizations. In recent years it has reached down to the housewife and individual consumer. Budgeting can be applied to the consumer just as well as to the industrialist who buys his machinery on credit. It comes to the aid of the home owner who pays for his home through the Coöperative Bank, or the Federal Housing Administration. Is not the consumer entitled to credit as well as the Government, which sold bonds on the instalment plan during the World War? This is the plea. Careful budgeting is stimulated where instalment sales come into the picture. Another angle is this: Some persons who have outstanding instalment payments may feel the responsibility of meeting their obligation.

Thus they may try to keep their jobs and work more steadily in order to have the income with which to pay. It is claimed that instalment buying has introduced thrift, in the form of a budget plan for managing household expenses, into homes where otherwise there would have been no systematic saving. If so, I have failed to find such a home.

9. As far as the business man is concerned it is pointed out that if he does not use instalment selling but carries on his business on an open-account basis, he risks having these accounts run indefinitely, or having them never paid. In such cases he has no longer

any claim on the merchandise purchased and cannot repossess it. On the other hand, instalment customers try to keep up their payments so as not to forfeit their purchases. If financial stress comes, the man with the open account may be more apt to delay payment than the man who has obligated himself by an instalment-payment contract. Open accounts are left to the last. The customer takes the stand that he will pay the bill whenever he can and the seller must bide his time. In case, however, customers should stop their payments on instalment purchases, then the company can repossess the merchandise. Some purchasers figure they have already had the use of the product for a while anyway.

10. This method of financing purchases affords a very easy method of handling payments. There is no chasing around trying to arrange suitable credit and security in order to make the purchase. All this is taken care of by the seller of the goods.

INSTALMENTS WIN CUSTOMERS

Sponsors of instalment plans assert that there has been little economic loss as a result of this method of selling. Prior to the 1929-1935 business depression, it was feared that small retail businesses would suffer greatly from unpaid accounts and returned goods; but it was not so. During that trying period a real effort was made by consumers to keep up such payments. The one thought seemed to be to meet these obligations so as not to lose the goods which had come to play such an important part in their everyday life.

That experience, however, as I have previously explained, does not prove that the instalment system is harmless. At certain periods in the business cycle, an expansion in "time" sales gives business an effective boost. At other times, however, such an expansion only helps to knock over the top-heavy credit pyramid.

It was hardly necessary to point out the above reasons for instalment selling. They have received great publicity, throughout the land, from sales organizations which have thought it to their advantage to sell on instalments. It is too bad that we have not had as much money spent in instructing the *consumer* on the reasons why he or she should not get entangled in instalment buying. If every dollar spent in urging instalment buying were matched with another dollar to point out the disadvantages, I am sure a great many prospective instalment customers would be guided away from the pitfalls of instalment buying. Let us now look at some of the disadvantages of buying on instalment.

ABUSES OF INSTALMENT PLANS

1. Instalment plans encourage the consumer to run into debt. He does not have the money with which to pay cash. He therefore buys with the belief that he will be able to meet his obligations as they come due. An instalment is a mortgage on one's future earnings—and who knows what his future earnings are to be? Who knows how permanent his job is? Who knows what his health will be in coming months? The future of all of us is as uncertain as the weather. We

expect a fair day tomorrow; but sudden squalls and tempests may arise. Both the weather forecaster and the business forecaster make mistakes. Forecasts are not infallible and they may be very wrong. The same is true of the man (or woman) who buys on the instalment plan. He buys today on the forecast of continued "fair weather" tomorrow, but the forecast may be misleading.

2. There is a growing tendency on the part of the younger generation today to demand new conditions under which to live. They expect the right to have luxuries which the financial condition of many homes does not justify. Instalment buying tends to make one a spendthrift. Too often the desire to *have* excites one to purchase more than he can swing. If there comes a time when you cannot carry on, then the instalment purchase is surrendered; and what is there to show for the payments already made? It is bad enough to have to pay for merchandise bought long after it has lost its newness. To have to make payments on merchandise that has been consumed or used up appears like punishment. Very often purchasing of goods on instalment results in loss to the consumer. Once a contract is signed there are no loopholes by which to escape. Either you pay, or else you lose everything,—not only the article but all the money already paid. Often the final payments are the hardest to meet. At this stage of the game loss of the product means a considerable financial loss as well.

3. Instalment buying leads to extravagance. This method of consumer buying makes it so easy to over-

buy. The first instalment purchase may be for an article of vast usefulness and of economic value. This obligation was easily met so why not make another one? Then follows the second instalment purchase, and the third, and so on. Each payment may be of small amount, but an accumulation of these small amounts runs into large totals and often beyond what the purchaser's current income can stand. Keeping up with the neighbors has always been a temptation. A down payment and so much a week may permit a family to cling to the bandwagon—but for how long? There is grave danger in every dollar tied up in the instalment contract. Extravagance is the downfall of many a plan which might otherwise have worked out successfully.

4. The quality of merchandise purchased on the instalment plan is not always the highest. Often the person who purchases a product on the instalment plan gets an article of inferior quality. The customer is generally price conscious. He has made up his mind that he wants a particular article, but where will he buy it? He has not the price to pay cash. He shops around until he finds the concern that offers him the best rates or the easiest payments. He thinks little of the quality at such a time. His mind is wholly pinned on cost. Appearance plays an important part in his selection, but like beauty it is sometimes only skin deep. This may result in the customer purchasing an article the payments for which continue beyond the life of the merchandise.

5. It is annoying enough to have small bills continu-

ally coming to hand. It is especially so if the goods have already been used up or have lost their newness and attractiveness. There has been a tendency sometimes to increase the down payments and shorten up on the length of time over which payments extend on these "perishable" products. Such a scheme is intended to overcome the objections of customers to making payments on a "dead horse." The finance people know it is to their advantage also to do this. If payments are defaulted, there is nothing left to repossess. When only a small down payment is required of a customer, he looks on his investment as a small item. But when the down payment amounts to, say, one-third of the total cost, then the customer thinks twice before risking the loss of both money and goods because of default. Larger down payments prevent some people from starting instalment accounts; but such larger payments may instil in the customer's mind the desire to meet the rest of his obligation.

6. Instalment purchases have lessened the volume of savings. It is true that savings are larger than in former years,[1] but if instalment selling had not played so important a part in recent years, the savings record of this country would be much larger. Instead of putting the money in the bank as *instalment savings* and receiving interest therefrom, consumers have been putting their money in financing institutions through *instalment selling* and paying interest thereon. Why

[1] In most banks this increase does not exceed the natural increase which comes from compound interest on the deposits.

not make use of the many savings clubs conducted by local banks? They provide depositors with vacation clubs, coal clubs, Christmas clubs, etc. These offer excellent facilities for saving money for a given purpose. A person knows in advance that he wants a vacation at a given time. He can plan for it and start saving. When the proper time comes he can go to the bank and withdraw his deposit with interest, for that purpose. Why not use the bank as your financing institution and cultivate thrift which has always been one of the foundation stones for success? If the finance companies are shortening the period over which payments can be made for a certain article, it would be far wiser to start saving an equivalent amount each week. Then at the end of the term period you can make a cash purchase. This is the way to buy economically. Cash purchases are the cheapest, safest and best.

Should you decide to save up for a washing machine, for example, put aside each month the amount which it would cost monthly in instalment payments. Put the money in the bank. You would not have to go without the article for any great length of time. You probably have done without that washing machine for some time already, and what is six or nine months longer? The worry entailed by those who are burdened with instalment payments sometimes leads to serious ends. It is said that "it is not hard work that kills a man, but worry." My suggestion is that the consumer should save first and spend after. Enjoy the feeling of being a saver as well as a cash-spender.

You will thereby save money and get better merchandise. In this connection there is presented an illustrative family budget under the title "A Plan for Working Your Money Instead of Letting the Instalment Crowd Work You."

7. There are some concerns whose methods of conducting instalment selling may be questionable. Would you rather do business with such concerns, or with a local bank where you know the individual officers and members handling the accounts, men whose soundness and integrity are under strict supervision? Some of the finance companies are encouraging instalment selling of commodities or even services—apparently merely that instalment paper may be created which they can discount at high rates. Some people think they pay no more for goods purchased on the instalment plan than if they paid cash or bought on credit. This is high folly. In another chapter of this book I point out what the customer *really* pays for the "privilege" of buying on terms. It is sufficient here to say that high carrying charges added to the long price of goods reduces the purchasing power of the consumer of such goods.

8. Buying some goods on the instalment plan tends to slow up payments due on other accounts. Instead of accepting the first of the month as "bill date" and whenever possible paying up promptly, instalment buyers become careless about their bills. Other accounts are side-tracked. Slow accounts have been a bugbear to many small retailers. The persistent cry has been to shorten up the time of outstanding bills.

A PLAN FOR WORKING YOUR MONEY INSTEAD OF LETTING THE INSTALMENT CROWD WORK YOU

*Income	Accumulation				Living Expenses						Benevolence & Church		Personal and Miscel.	
	%	Insurance	Sav. Bank and Invest.	Speculative Fund	%	Food	Clothes	%	Housing	Trans.	%	Am't	%	Am't
$1,200	8	$14	$24	$0	46	$410	$140	38	$400	$50	1	$12	12	$150
1,500	6	35	40	0	43	475	175	35	440	80	2	25	15	230
2,000	8	80	80	0	39½	550	240	33½	500	170	2½	50	16½	330
2,500	11	135	135	0	36½	600	290	33½	575	250	3	85	17	430
3,000	13	190	190	0	52½	640	330	33½	640	370	4	120	17	520
3,500	15	210	310	0	29	650	370	33½	730	450	4½	160	18	620
4,000	15	220	390	0	28½	680	455	34	845	510	5	200	17½	700
5,000	20	265	370	350	24	710	510	32	1,005	600	6	300	18	890
7,500	25½	400	600	770	21½	920	690	29	1,420	750	8	600	18	1,350
10,000	27½	600	1,030	1,140	18½	1,050	780	30	2,000	1,000	9	900	15	1,500
12,500	28	750	1,350	1,400	15	1,070	830	30	2,500	1,200	10	1,250	17	2,150
15,000	30½	1,050	1,730	1,830	13½	1,130	910	30	3,000	1,500	11	1,650	15	2,220
20,000	31½	1,400	2,300	2,530	11½	1,300	1,020	32	4,450	2,000	12	2,400	13	2,600
25,000	31½	1,350	3,150	3,350	9½	1,400	1,050	33	5,900	2,300	13	3,250	13	3,250
30,000	33	1,400	3,900	4,700	9	1,500	1,100	32	6,850	2,750	13	3,900	13	3,900
40,000	33	1,800	6,300	7,300	8	1,800	1,300	27	7,300	3,400	16	6,400	11	4,400
50,000	40	2,500	8,500	9,200	7	1,950	1,450	27	9,400	4,000	16	8,000	10	5,000

*Net after income taxes and social security, and for family of 4 people, of which two are young children.

Insurance — Calculated on maximum death benefit, i.e. ordinary life.

Investment — Funds placed for income primarily in savings banks or in investment securities.

Speculative Fund — Funds placed for income primarily with expectation of profit.

Housing — Rent and/or taxes, interest, repairs, upkeep and heat; also service and house servants, light, cooking fuel and ice expenses, home equipment and replacements. Housing and Transportation are mutually related.

They may be added together and considered as a unit.

Transportation — Carfares, travel fund and/or automobile depreciation and expense.

Personal and Miscellaneous — Education, and school fund, recreation, medical care and other personal expenses.

Apparently there had been considerable headway made in this direction.   But instalment sales are adversely affecting this drive for short-term open accounts. When income is limited, collections are behind on regular charge accounts, due to the necessity of meeting payments under the instalment plan.   If the buying public could be induced to use good judgment, then instalment buying would not be so unhealthy.   However, it is unfortunate that a large proportion of consumers are not of the sort to budget their requirements. They do not know what they will have available as time goes on.   They act more upon impulse than upon good judgment.

9. Instalment selling increases the cost of distribution severely.   The hue and cry in recent years has been that the high cost of goods is largely due to the high cost of distribution.   If this statement is true, then the object of every business man should be to reduce the cost of distribution.   Research and experimenting have been going on in practically every industry to find the most efficient way of reducing distribution costs so that the goods will be priced within the reach of more consumers.   In the face of such a nationwide endeavor why should instalment selling be advocated?   Many sales made on the instalment plan add materially to the cost of the product.   The details of collecting payments and bookkeeping, although small in percentage, are in the aggregate increasing the costs of distribution instead of lowering them.   If merchandise is repossessed, here is another expense to the company.   Losses from bad debts must also be

figured into the distribution costs which a customer eventually pays. It is very uneconomic to sell on the instalment plan commodities which deteriorate rapidly and which would be difficult to recover should the debtor default.

10. Some industries suffer at the expense of others. Anyone knows that if a person ties himself up with payments on a washing machine, automobile, jewelry, or what-not, he is no longer a prospect for many essentials such as clothing, food, shoes, etc. Most instalment buying generally involves purchases of considerable dollar volume. Such obligations limit the remaining purchases one can make. Instalment selling may temporarily help automobile, electric-refrigerator, washing-machine, and fur-coat industries, for example. Simultaneously other industries are penalized by scarcity of purchasing power.

PYRAMIDING BRINGS DISASTER

The over-extension of time-payment plans is an unhealthy development. While a person may mortgage his property within reason a man should not mortgage his future income unless absolutely compelled to do so and then only temporarily. Urging the buyer into debt by instalment-plan buying is bound to create trouble, discontent and unhappiness. Instalment buying or debt contracting by poor people is a calamity. It places a mortgage upon their health, their jobs and their earning power. It creates as much unhappiness, misery and discontent as any other bad habit.

The company which sells on an instalment plan

should learn definitely and specifically what other outstanding credit contracts the customer has before selling him further. It has been the custom for a long time for some companies to require written statements as to the credit standing of prospective buyers. But it seems to me the most important questions are: How many *other* items is the customer buying on credit? To what extent do these tie up his future income?

In the development of instalment sales, undesirable tendencies have occasionally manifested themselves. Certain merchants, manufacturers and finance companies, in their desire to get more business, have been guilty of laying aside proper standards of credit requirements. Sometimes they have accepted smaller cash payments than should be required, or have extended the terms of payment beyond a reasonable length of time. There is foolish instalment *selling* as well as foolish instalment *buying*. Every concern which sells merchandise through an instalment plan has a moral obligation to the people. It is up to the seller to prevent an over-extension of this form of credit; over-extension is the ruination of many customers.

CHAPTER FIVE

WHAT BUYING ON INSTALMENTS COSTS CONSUMERS

"Living upon trust is the best way to pay double."—*Stone*

Instalment buyers remind me somewhat of a kid I used to know as "Precious." That, of course, was the boy's nickname. He was a good kid and the idol of his mother's heart. Possibly he has long since forgiven her for hanging on him such a sissy nickname. Naturally, a boy who allowed his mother to call him "Precious" was not especially popular with our gang. Nevertheless, the lad would rather play with us than do anything else—except ride his bicycle. Since that bicycle was the only one in the neighborhood, it made the gang envious. So we used to say to Precious: "We'll let you play with us tomorrow if you'll let us ride your bicycle." After much hesitation, he would finally yield: "Well, just for around the block; that's all." But that did not satisfy the gang, and we did not stop working on him until we had wheedled that bike out of him for at least a half-day. Considering our rough treatment of it, and the little that he got in return, Precious said he understood what Benjamin Franklin meant when he wrote about paying "too much for the whistle."

Credit, in the case of the instalment buyer, is the

whistle for which he pays too much. But the sad part of it is that he himself apparently does not think so. This is evidenced by the fact that instalment credit has increased by leaps and bounds during the past twenty years, reaching an estimated peak in 1929 of $6,500,000,000. This figure represented 13.2% of total retail sales for that year. In 1936, estimated instalment sales totaled $4,500,000,000—a sharp drop from the 1929 peak, but still a tidy sum. Instalment sales in 1937, according to the U. S. Department of Commerce, amounted to approximately $4,950,000,000, or 12.25% of the year's estimated total retail sales. Thus the instalment buyer is still convinced that his whistle is well worth the price, despite the fact that he pays for it by an increase of around 11% or more added to the normal price, depending upon the length of time the instalments run and the terms imposed.

INSTALMENT INCENTIVES

The astounding success of instalment plans, notwithstanding their usurious cost, is accounted for by the temperament of our Western world. Most Americans "want what they want when they want it," whether or not they have the ready cash with which to pay for it. They are surrounded on every side by the marvelous and alluring products of the world's greatest technical genius. They feel what Kipling in his poem, *The American Spirit,* has called "the instant need of things." They are averse to counting the cost, so long as they can have *today* that which prudence would patiently wait for until tomorrow. This is an un-

certain age; and tomorrow may never come. Therefore, why wait? And wait they do not. They sign
today on the dotted line for that trim electric refrigerator, that efficient-looking washing machine, that
shining new automobile. They put down anywhere
from 10% to 33⅓% as the case may be. They obli-
gate themselves to pay the balance in instalments
extending over periods of a few months to as much as
three years. To the "small carrying charge," which
the salesman, with consummate tact, usually mentions
sotto voce, they give little attention, at first. Later,
they may have occasion to consider it seriously.

The typically American disease known as putting
up a front also tends to aggravate the instalment
fever. It obscures, in the minds of many, the fact
that time purchases entail a severe monetary penalty.
If one family buys a new car, the family next door
begins to regard its own car with growing disfavor.
The outcome, of course, is a new car for nearly
everybody in the neighborhood—bought on the instalment plan. No matter if some budgets are already
badly strained; even the impecunious must have the
new cars anyway in order to hold their heads up before
the world. This procedure is repeated in millions of
homes throughout the country, not only in the case of
automobiles, but in that of the numerous other articles
that are sold on the instalment plan.

MISLEADING CHARGES

Let us in this chapter get down to brass tacks, to
the cost to consumers of instalment buying. The cost

angle centers in what merchants almost invariably refer to as "a small carrying charge." Accuracy, if not honesty, would be better served if the adjective were omitted. The cost of instalment credit, as we shall soon see in some detail, is anything but small. This is true despite the fact that carrying charges have dropped materially in recent years. The average today is around 6%.

On the face of it, a 6% carrying charge looks innocent enough. It amounts, as any instalment-store salesman will tell you with anticipatory affability, to only one-half of one per cent a month. That, of course, is the truth; for one-half of one per cent a month, in any man's arithmetic, is 6% a year. Just where, then, does Shylock enter, demanding his pound of flesh?

When the consumer signs the usual instalment agreement, he obligates himself to pay back each month one-twelfth of the total amount of his bill as it stands after the initial down payment. However, he continues to pay the fixed rate of interest on the *entire original* principal amount of the note. Although he reduces his indebtedness by one-twelfth each month, he pays interest at the *full* rate for the time on *twelve-twelfths*. This is as fine an example as we have seen of getting nothing for something. Obviously, when the consumer, under this sort of financing, pays interest on money that he does not owe, the rate on the money that he does owe is correspondingly jacked up. Thus this innocent-looking 6% jumps with remarkable alacrity to about an 11% per annum basis on the average loan outstanding, when the payments are spread over a full year. This rate per annum may be considerably higher when the payment period is different. Even an amateur economist knows that credit at these rates is a very expensive whistle.

TWO INTERESTING ANGLES

It is the practice of some stores to advertise that they make no interest charge on instalment purchases. The instalment buyer should not be deceived by this technique. In all probability the carrying charge has been concealed in the price of the merchandise. Such stores usually offer a discount for cash. This means, in effect, that the purchaser is paying 10% or more for instalment accommodation. A 10% carrying charge makes just as big a hole in the consumer's pocketbook whether it is hidden in loaded prices or is the result of "an open covenant, openly arrived at."

Here is another interesting angle to the carrying charge. Mr. Consumer is paying off an instalment account at the rate of fifteen dollars a month. He operates on a close economic margin, and has very little money even for necessities. It so happens that Mrs. Consumer needs a new dress or the family car needs a new tire; but just at this crucial time another instalment falls due. Instead, therefore, of paying the full fifteen dollars, Mr. Consumer pays only five, and with the remaining ten buys the dress or the tire. This transaction places him ten dollars in default on the instalment account. What happens? The company, being a strictly business organization, must conduct its affairs in strictly business fashion. It figures that eleven months will elapse before that ten dollars is paid, unless extra payments are made in the meantime. Interest at 6% on ten dollars, for eleven months, amounts to fifty-five cents. This is added to Mr. Consumer's indebtedness. But what is fifty-five cents compared to a new frock for Mrs. Consumer or a new tire for the family bus?

SOME SPECIFIC EXAMPLES

A few specific examples will serve to emphasize the high cost of credit to the instalment buyer. Furniture is as good as anything to begin with. Some concerns have sold on a financing plan of one-half of one per cent a month on the balance after the initial down payment. Your purchase amounts, say, to $100. You pay $10 down and sign an agreement to pay the remaining $90 in twelve equal payments of $7.50 each. For this privilege you are charged $5.40—the interest on $90 for one year at 6%. Of course, you have not borrowed the full $90 for a full year, but only for one month. After the lapse of that first month, your outstanding indebtedness has been reduced by $7.50 to $82.50. The second month it is further reduced by $7.50 to $75; and so on by $7.50 each month until the debt is fully discharged. Yet you continue to pay interest at 6% per annum on the *original* amount of your indebtedness. As a result, the real rate of interest figures up to over 11%.

A sewing machine of a certain make sells for $83.10 cash and $96 on time. On this machine the consumer pays $10 down and the balance in monthly instal-

ments of $5. The interest rate on the money actually
lent figures up to about 20% per annum. Another
machine of the same company sells for $117.30 cash,
and $138 on time. The down payment is $25; the
balance is due in monthly instalments of $10. The
interest rate in this case amounts to approximately
25%. Two competing vacuum cleaners draw down
finance charges of 11.5% and 21.8% respectively. A
well-known washing machine will reach into the consumer's pocketbook for financing charges varying from
12% to 30%, depending upon the length of time over
which the payments continue.

AND SO IT GOES

There may be no point in multiplying examples, but
here are a few more. They are presented just in case
you are not yet convinced that Franklin's saying with
respect to paying too dearly for his whistle is equally
applicable to instalment-plan buying. One of many
electric refrigerators of a certain large company cost
$179.50 if purchased for cash. This same model, if
purchased on a thirty-six-month time-payment basis,
would cost $207, or $27.50 more than the cash price—
an increase in cost of over 15%. But it is your money,
and if you insist on spending it that way, who is to
stop you?

Perhaps you are tired of stoking the old furnace
and have decided to buy an oil burner. You can purchase one of a certain type for $300 cash. Since your
bank-roll is a little thin at the moment, you go down
town and buy this same burner on the instalment plan.

At the rate of $9.68 a-payment, your total cost is
$348.48, or $48.48 more than the cash price.   Here,
again, the increase in cost is around 15%.   But what
is that compared to the present convenience of pushing
a button or turning a small wheel on that thermostat
out in the hall!

What about jewelry?   If you purchase an article in
a credit store, you will pay the same price in most
instances, whether you buy on a cash or a credit basis.
In some cases, when you buy on the instalment plan,
the store will give you coupons equal to one-twentieth
or 5% of your payments.   These coupons can be used
only in purchasing the equivalent cash amount of merchandise in that same store.   If you pay cash, it is
possible, in some cases, to get a 5% discount from the
list price.   This type of store usually does not do business on a cash basis, and hence can mark the prices on
all its goods on an instalment-selling basis.   More
specifically, a ring listed at fifty dollars in a credit
store can be purchased for considerably less than
forty dollars in a cash store.   On the other hand, if
you purchase a fifty-dollar ring on a time-payment
basis, you will pay for it about 30% more than the
fifty-dollar cash price.

"PAYING AS YOU RIDE"

The outstanding example of instalment buying is in
the automobile field.   Automobile financing got under
way on a small scale as long ago as 1915, when John
North Willys formed a finance company to push the
sales of Overland cars.   Four years later, General

Motors launched the General Motors Acceptance Corporation. By 1922, when the motor era had just about begun, this financing concern, and Commercial Investment Trust, and Commercial Credit were all well under way. Many other smaller finance companies sprang up throughout the country. The profit lure was strong. Charges of from 1% to 2% a month of the initial balance were the rule. The current rate is ½% a month on new cars and about ¾% on used cars. The succeeding years were marked by continued growth of automobile sales financing. In 1937, I believe that about 60% of the new cars were sold on the instalment plan. They were bought, for the most part, by people making from thirty to sixty dollars a week.

Up until the summer of 1937, you could get very liberal terms from the automobile finance companies. So anxious were they for the business, that they would write contracts giving you two years in which to pay. Later, however, the whole industry restricted its terms to 33⅓% down, with a limit of eighteen equal monthly payments on cars less than two years old. On older cars, the practice is to demand 33⅓% plus twelve equal monthly payments.

The present method of automobile financing is known as the "six per cent financing plan." Admitting the fact that it reduces the cost of financing the deferred balance by about 25%, as compared with earlier methods, I nevertheless hold no brief in its favor. It is still costly to "pay as you ride." In the spring of 1937, a young man I know was driving a 1932 roadster of a certain popular make. It was a good little car, but his hankering for a new one finally got the best of him. So he shopped around for the highest turn-in allowance on the roadster. By pitting one dealer against another, and buying toward the fag end of the automobile season, he succeeded in getting the allowance jacked up to $204. This was accepted as the down payment on a new car costing $654. Terms still being liberal, he signed a contract to pay the balance of $450 in twenty-four equal monthly instalments of $18.75 each, at a financing charge of ½% a month on that total amount. The cost to him was $54 which figured out to approximately 11.58%. This made the total cost of his new car $708, instead of $654. The former figure is exclusive, of course, of any amount which is invariably charged for insurance against fire and theft hazards.

In 1937, 4,122,750 automobiles were sold in the United States. Sixty per cent of them, or 2,473,650, were sold on the instalment plan. Suppose, for the sake of illustration, that the average finance charge on each car amounted to the figure mentioned in the preceding paragraph, namely, $54. It might have been less; it might have been more. At that figure, the total cost of financing these 2,473,650 cars aggregated the huge sum of $133,577,100. Is it any wonder the income accounts of the leading finance companies make easy reading? That money would have purchased 204,246 new automobiles at $654 each. It is the equivalent of a per capita annual family tax of about $5.00. This would support an army of unemployed for some time. "Paying as you ride" is obviously a great economic waste.

WHAT YOU PAY FOR

It is axiomatic that in this world you seldom, if ever, get something for nothing. If you insist on buying on the instalment plan, you must expect to have passed along to you the materially increased costs of doing business on the instalment basis. That they are substantial is indicated by the fact that in the home-furnishings field the operating expenses of retail stores depending on instalment sales are from 35% to 45% of sales. This is substantially above the operating expenses of retail stores in that field which are conducted on the ordinary retail basis.

The operation of a credit department may necessitate additional office space and the employment of extra help, such as stenographers, accountants, and a credit manager. Reserves must be set up to take care of losses on bad accounts. Legal talent must be engaged. Warehousing, delivery, freight and express expenses run high. Household furniture, musical instruments, oil burners, electric washing machines, and many other items usually sold on the instalment plan are bulky. The expenses of handling them are correspondingly large. Advertising costs of instalment stores are also likely to be heavier than in other types of retail stores. The reason is plain. Instalment sales cannot be maintained at high levels unless the public is constantly bombarded with appeals through the press and over the radio to purchase goods on the instalment plan.

Hammer at them hard enough and long enough, and the public will submit to the slavery of indebtedness without a murmur. Advertising managers of credit houses know this, and play it up for all it is worth. It costs money, of course, but they figure on getting it all back again through the carrying charge. As stated before, you are the goat. You pay for the whole instalment set-up and a large profit in addition. The carrying charge, therefore, does not represent true interest, but is more in the nature of a service charge. The high rates include both interest on the money borrowed, plus an additional amount for services rendered. The effect on your pocketbook, however, is the same, whatever terminology be employed to describe the charges. To what extent instalment houses make a net profit on the carrying charges is a moot point. There are responsible students of the subject who maintain that "there is a net profit in the instalment charge over and above actual expenses and average risks."

OTHER NEEDLESS COSTS

The financing charges are not the only costs to the instalment buyer. Instalment sales, as we have already seen, run into huge figures. The cost of financing this mountainous debt represents a direct levy on the purchasing power of the consumer. Since the money he spends on buying credit might have been saved and later used to purchase goods for cash, he definitely lowers his standard of living. In other words, by spending money for credit that should, or could, go into merchandise, he suffers a certain material deprivation that is tantamount to a reduced living standard. In the aggregate, the living standard of the American people is seriously handicapped by their mania for instalment buying.

The nation's instalment debt annually amounts to over \$5,000,000,000. If payments, on the average, were extended over a period of twelve months, the carrying charges on this sum would amount, at $\frac{1}{2}$ of 1% a month, to \$297,000,000,—equivalent to a per capita annual family tax of over \$10. Think of the amount of merchandise that \$297,000,000 could buy! How many vacuum cleaners, how many oil burners, how many washing machines, how many automobiles! Surely the consumer is rightly characterized as foolish when he spends his substance in this way for that which is not bread. He might just as well have thrown that money to the four winds for all the good it did him.

The high cost of instalment buying is an economic waste that is scarcely compensated for by any alleged benefits that may flow from it. The consumer would be far better off if each week or month he would set aside in the bank a stipulated sum, to be used finally for the cash purchase of some product. By so doing he would get an automobile, an electric refrigerator, an oil burner, a vacuum cleaner, or whatever other merchandise he desires in a more modern type and for less money. In this way he would avoid the heavy carrying charges and, in many instances, get the benefit of sizable cash discounts. Furthermore, he would receive interest on his savings, instead of paying exorbitant interest on. his borrowings.

Such a cash purchaser would also escape the danger of over-extension and the suffering which such indebtedness frequently entails. But it takes courage and sacrifice to practice instalment saving. It seems easier for the average American to live today and die tomorrow than to enrich tomorrow's living by sacrificing today. So it is that the instalment merry-go-round whirls dizzily on. Unless its speed is carefully controlled, some day the merry-go-round will break down, the brass ring will turn to cast-iron, and the music will become a sorry symphony of distress.

FACTOR OF OBSOLESCENCE

Then there is to be considered the factor of obsolescence. Frequently, obsolescence destroys values faster than use wears them out. This is particularly true of devices which are subject to rapid and repeated improvement. Take, for example, radios. The radio industry has made remarkable progress in recent years, and is still forging ahead with indefatigable zeal. As a result, the radio of a few years ago is as out of date today as last year's popular songs. By the same token, today's radio will be rendered just as obsolete by the product of tomorrow. Technical genius in the radio industry, as well as in other industries, is constantly at work making obsolescence more effective. New things for new dollars is the *leitmotif* of the modern laboratory. No doubt many of my readers have stored away in their cellars discarded radios which were purchased a few years ago at a high price on the instalment plan. These old models have been supplanted by the many-gadgeted new models of today.

Obsolescence is constantly taking its toll, and you, Mr. Consumer, are the victim. If, therefore, you must buy on the instalment plan, at least guard against purchasing on that basis articles which the factor of obsolescence will shortly render practically valueless. Also take care that you, at all times, buy quality, rather than patronize the store granting the most liberal terms, regardless of quality. It is not particularly pleasant to be forced to continue payments on, say, a suite of furniture that begins to break up before the final instalment falls due. Instalment buying is costly in any event, but doubly so under certain conditions.

A GALLING YOKE

Most instalment buyers undoubtedly make their commitments in good faith. In fact, of many it may be said that they have more faith than vision. They buy on the basis of present and expected future income. They fully intend to make their payments regularly until their debt is settled. For this they are to be commended. But usually they make no allowance for contingencies. As I have already remarked, people forget that economic weather is ever changing. They assume that things will continue in the even tenor of their present way. Never was there a period when that assumption had so little basis as it has today.

These are strenuous times. Change is the order of the day. The mere fact that a man is now working is no guarantee that he will be working six months from now. He may be setting aside a little money today, and six months hence be pounding the pavements looking for a job that does not exist. Modern life is like that. We can recall what it did to thousands in 1929 and the years that immediately followed. Again in 1937 there was experienced within a few months one of the sharpest business recessions in history. Many were then thrown into idleness, or dependence upon government aid for the pittances they received. Prior to the business setback they had no inkling that their lot would undergo such drastic change. Perhaps most people do not care very much what tomorrow may bring forth, so long as they can have today their heart's desire. Yet, when income stops, or is materially reduced, the "easy payments" of the instalment buyer may become a galling yoke. In fact, an instalment buyer's income may continue at its accustomed level and a disastrous result take place. I refer to the possibility of his own, or his family's sudden illness. Some other unforeseen emergency may demand unusual expenditures that make it difficult, if not impossible, to continue instalment payments.

TRAGEDY OF REPOSSESSION

Of these circumstances I have already written in a previous chapter. I, however, do want you to remember that when you buy goods on the instalment plan, you vest title with the seller or the finance company. The goods do not become yours until the final instalment is paid. You merely rent them until you are handed a receipt in full. Since the instalment contract is really a lease, with provisions for a conditional sale if, and when, all payments are made, the penalty for default of payment is repossession of the goods. Of course, you may possibly get an extension; but if the worst comes you will lose not only the goods, but the payments that you have made on them. Meanwhile possibly you will have undergone considerable hounding for payment, with all the mental anguish that such treatment inevitably entails. It is decidedly unjust for a furniture store, say, to repossess goods for which you have paid in full. But let me illustrate.

Suppose that you have purchased on the instalment plan a living-room suite, a dining-room suite, and a bed-room suite, each costing $150, or a total of $450.

Instead of signing a separate contract for each of these sets, you sign a single contract for all three of them; that is, you bind yourself for a single contract of $450, rather than for three separate contracts of $150 each. You make your monthly payments regularly until you have paid, say, $300. Then, through no fault of your own, you lose your job and are unable to continue any payments whatsoever. What does the furniture store do? Does it allow you to keep two of the three sets for which you have paid in full? By no means. It sends out its van and carts away all three sets! Could anything be more unjust than that?

If instalment selling is to continue, the laws governing it should be so revised as to enable the buyer to keep, when things go wrong, the goods for which he has already paid. This should be irrespective of the fact that they were purchased under a single contract. As it is, the instalment buyer pays too much for his whistle, without being subjected to such unconscionable robbery.

May I offer the following suggestions to those who will continue to buy on the instalment plan despite this book:

1. Pay cash for comparatively small purchases, since the cost of financing them is proportionately high. 2. Bear in mind the fact that any article that rapidly depreciates entails a high finance charge. 3. Buy on instalments only articles the price and quality of which are widely publicized. By observing these rules you will protect yourself from hidden mark-ups in the finance charge. Better still: *Do not purchase any article on instalments, but practice instalment saving.* Thereby you will pay for your whistle exactly what it is worth and no more.

CHAPTER SIX

RELATION OF INSTALMENT BUYING TO MARKETS AND EMPLOYMENT

"I have discovered the philosopher's stone that turns everything into gold. It is 'pay as you go.'"—*John Randolph*

> "Simple Simon met a pie-man
> Going to the fair.
> Said Simple Simon to the pie-man,
> 'Let me taste your ware.'
> Said the pie-man to Simple Simon,
> 'Show me first your penny!'
> Said Simple Simon to the pie-man,
> 'Indeed I have not any.'"

So runs the nursery rhyme that we all learned as children. Under the "dollar-down-and-dollar-a-week" philosophy of instalment selling, the hero of our nursery jingle need not have been greatly embarrassed for the means of tasting this pastry delicacy. Whether or not he would continue to pay for his gourmet satisfaction after the enjoyment became but a memory, is another question! Advocates of more or less unlimited instalment plans would claim that Young Simon was doing his bit to build up mass consumption as a counterbalance to mass production. Therefore, they would argue that he aided in minimizing the unemployment valleys of the business cycle.

I doubt very much the practical efficacy of that theory. By carrying this method of distribution to an extreme, we are developing a means of milking the working class dry. We are courting inflation of the worst kind. We are encouraging the fool to part with his money for years to come. I grant that in the early days of a period of inflation a large debtor class is contracting for future obligations which *theoretically* it may be able to pay off with cheaper dollars. *Actually*, however, the great middle class is always the principal sufferer under any such radical change in monetary values. Historically it has never shown the sagacity and energy to safeguard itself against inflationary pitfalls,—and these are legion.

ROBBING PETER TO PAY PAUL

People will say that "luxury" is a relative term, that shoes are a luxury in countries where the inhabitants go barefooted. It is contended that instalment plans enable the wage earner to live on the fat of the land and enjoy the proverbial "more abundant life." Even on the wild assumption that this is true, the cost of such prodigality would be tremendous. As a matter of cold fact abnormal exploitation of instalment sales merely robs the future cash market. I reiterate the obvious fact that the instalment injection is temporarily stimulating. It may result, however, in ultimate weakness for the entire business and credit structure of any country which resorts to such a perilous artifice. Any debt is large or small in relation to one's ability to pay. As an example, take 1937, a year when business was nearly normal. At that time the volume of instalment contracts we have estimated at between 5% and 6% of the national income of approximately $70,000,000,000. Admittedly that volume of consumer credit was not out of proportion. The idea can, moreover, gather momentum and size, similar to a rolling snowball. The spread of time sales into the "consumer goods" field is particularly dangerous for this reason. Nobody likes to pay for a "dead horse." At least, in buying an automobile the article has some value when the last payment is made. The second-hand value of a pair of pants, however, is extremely dubious. The clothing industry may build up for itself a lot of future grief by unduly liberalizing its credit relationship with the public.

There is naturally a great difference between the volume of instalment selling and the amount of unpaid instalment debt. A borrower who owes a balance on a large purchase is obviously in a better position than the borrower who owes the same amount on a smaller purchase. The former has built up equity value which he may be expected to try to protect; while the only claim a seller has on the smaller buyer is his signature on notes. This signature may have little value if the buyer over-hypothecates his future earnings.

Extensive instalment selling assumes a steady level of income and a budget for the salaried man that is contingent upon continued prosperity. Actually the only time that wages, either when rising or falling, ever catch up with prices is at the end of a cycle.

Even then, after a relatively short time, prices begin to move in the opposite direction.

Taking 1937 as an illustration, the average American family then was meeting a monthly instalment payment of $26 to secure a title to goods which it was enjoying. It may be claimed that an average consumer indebtedness of this amount is not a dangerous condition, even if consideration is given to possibilities of business recession. It is argued—and plausibly—that the effect of such a debt would be relatively small, especially if the notes outstanding at any one time mature serially. Hence, it is contended, these notes can be paid off despite any period of declining income, or even unemployment. Experience tends to confirm this observation. The question however is this: *Can a satisfactory record of collections be continued if it becomes possible to buy all kinds of goods and services on the instalment plan, as seems likely?*

Statistics indicate that the average instalment contract entered into during a normal year is paid off in seven months. Presumably that should not be too dangerous a situation inasmuch as the borrower can liquidate his payments in less than a year. *It is the trend that is dangerous, however.*

FINANCE COMPANIES' THEORY

The finance companies appear to operate on the following theory. They seem to assume that long terms and small down payments are justified during a period of subnormal business activity, such as 1932. They evidently feel that shorter terms and larger down payments are desirable as business advances above normal, or during a period such as the spring of 1937, to point to a specific situation. The logic behind this reasoning is based on the fact that when business is sliding off, instalment-credit sales drop faster than either open-credit sales or cash sales; and that cash sales decline relatively the least.

In other words, experience has indicated that during hard times the instalment buyer is more conservative than either the consumer who buys on thirty days' credit or the consumer who buys for cash. Theoretically, therefore, the contention is that an instalment sale made in a period of depression should be sound. At such a time, it is maintained, the consumer does not dare involve himself in purchases which are not essential. Furthermore, the credit giver does not dare accept the risk unless he can be absolutely convinced that the recipient of the credit is worthy and will pay.

The records show that the majority of the finance companies tightened up during the spring of 1937 on their credit liens covering new motor car purchases. In the light of history it appears evident that during the latter part of 1936 credit should not have been extended so freely. When the Roosevelt Administration made a statement to the effect that retail prices were too high in March 1937, the credit condition was not healthy. The basis was then being laid for the sudden business recession, which later ensued.

Therefore, there should be nothing excessively perilous about instalment buying *if* a safe percentage of the consumer public could be depended upon to use good judgment. Unfortunately, however, a large proportion of consumers are not the type to budget their requirements. Thus they are unable to decide just what resources they will have available as time goes on. They act more upon impulse than upon good judgment. They project an element of nervousness and uncertainty into the business picture. As a result, *easy money* can very quickly develop *uneasy business conditions*. It may contribute to a crisis, in which commercial failures will take place; firms shut down one after another, toppling like dominoes set in a row. That is, consumer debt may become one of the major causes of business depressions.

In view of such considerations as the above it appears probable that a rather large part of instalment buying is not being conducted on a sufficiently conservative basis. In my opinion it is not a development along truly normal and prudent lines. The better-than-average profits obtainable in the field have attracted some finance companies of unstable character. These are not in a favorable position to compete with the established concerns on a basis of service charges. These marginal firms may be tempted to extend terms on an unsound basis as competition becomes increasingly severe.

CONSUMER "CAMEL'S BACK"

I maintain that finance companies should study more carefully the load of debt which an applicant may already be carrying. No matter what the income of the purchaser may be, the instalment-purchase arrangement will permit him to live above his income for a certain length of time. If, during a period of adversity, he cannot meet his payments, trouble impends. The oil-burner man, the refrigerator salesman, the furniture dealer, and the automobile finance company all come in for repossessions. The back of the consumer camel may eventually be broken. A financial loss may be suffered by the sellers. The market may find it difficult to absorb the repossessed articles. The consumer himself faces an unfortunate plight in finding himself suddenly bereft of modern conveniences that he has become educated to look upon as necessities. Such are the natural reactions of overdoing the instalment business.

In a good many cases, financing charges are uneconomic. If the consumer's sales resistance is weak he can build up a burden that will actually lower his standard of living. He will get a smaller value for a given expenditure, as more of his outlay may be spent for credit, less for merchandise. Furthermore, during a period of increasing productivity, stimulated by instalment sales, industry will turn out a larger volume of production than can be absorbed. By overestimating the potential market, an inventory glut is created. Prices of course must be slashed. The condition is then ripe for the beginning of a deflationary spiral; this can rapidly be accelerated by repossessions resulting from defaulted instalment contracts.

A ROPE AROUND TOMORROW'S NECK

Instalment credit has been defined as a method by which families of limited income can *today* purchase the luxuries of *yesterday*, by pledging a part of *tomorrow's* earnings. Probably this definition is technically correct. Actually, however, are we not creating a situation whereby the following little anecdote may become a real possibility?

"My dear," said the old man tenderly, "today is our golden wedding day, and I have a little surprise for you."

"Yes?" asked his silver-haired wife.

He took her hand in his. "You see this engagement ring I gave you fifty-two·years ago."

"Yes?" said the old lady expectantly.

"Well, I paid the final instalment on it today, and I am proud to announce that it is now altogether yours!"

INSTALMENT CONTRACTS DURING THE NEXT DEPRESSION

Probably the great problem always facing the instalment-selling field is the effect which a prolonged period of depression will have upon payments. As stated previously, the volume of instalment selling follows the employment curve quite closely. Consumers are tempted during good times to buy up to the limit of their income. Thus a false base of prosperity is created. Once business hits "heavy weather" the defaults, repossessions, and contraction of production hasten the trend towards receding economic activity.

The principal customer of the finance companies is the $30-$60 per week salaried employee. I doubt very much that this individual can be relied upon to utilize his newly found credit rating wisely. Defenders of the instalment plans rely upon what I have already stated, viz.: The amount of instalment credit outstanding during a period of approximately normal business does not exceed 7% of the estimated annual income of the country. Such income is represented by salaries, wages, dividends, etc. Hence critics of the instalment business may be accused of building up a "bogey man" out of thin air. However, to use the words of Caillaux, former Premier of France, "The prophet of disaster is never popular. I still hold, however, that he who would help his fellow-men, can do so in a real sense only if, when he sees clouds arising in the distance, he points out untiringly and at no matter what cost to himself, how they may be dispersed."

If our same $30-$60 a week worker ups his instalment purchase to from 15% to 20% of his income, he is headed to build for himself a proverbial house of cards. That house may tumble spectacularly during a period of falling wages.

GOODS ON INSTALMENTS—U. S. STOCKS ON MARGIN

I maintain that in the field of retail trade, therefore, this potentially dangerous credit device will bear watching. It could create a situation which might eventually become similar to that surrounding the stock market in the fall of 1929. As a matter of fact, *the purchaser of consumer goods under an instalment contract is in a similar position to the speculator who sells the stock market short.* In the latter case, the individual sells what he does not own and defers delivery. In the former case, the individual accepts immediate delivery and defers payment. The creditor is protected in the case of stocks as the seller puts up the cash to indemnify the lender of the stock until he makes final sale. The creditor is protected in the case of household appliances by retaining title until the borrower completes his payments.

Although credit has been for years one of the foundation stones upon which modern business is built, it has been employed mainly in the financing of production. Instalment-selling credit becomes a means of financing consumption. Unquestionably it has crystallized the earning power of the average American family into a great new economic force. Can that force be kept within reasonable channels? Or will it some day cause devastating flood damage?

It is interesting to note that during certain periods when instalment purchases have increased there has been a substantial advance in the volume of savings bank deposits, life insurance, income and wages, home building, and security purchases. This would appear to indicate that this new method of distribution has developed thus far without too many growing pains. However, the cushion of safety is more illusory than real. This is because the wage earner is placed in the position where he can be affected in two ways by any partial collapse of this selling device. A person caught in an instalment contract is pinched by the two jaws of a vise. These two jaws are as follows:

(1) As a consumer, he is encouraged to buy articles that he should not own until he has saved a sufficient amount for their purchase outright. Therefore, he piles up an overhead that he can meet only when all conditions are favorable. This requires that his income must remain steady. He must also be fortunate enough to avoid those extraordinary expenses contingent upon sickness and death—exigencies which at sometime or other we all must face.

(2) As a unit in the cost of production he stands to suffer partial or complete unemployment or salary reductions. This is the common story, coming at a time when the volume of new instalment contracts decreases. The wheels of production must be slowed down in order to liquidate burdensome inventories. The glut has been created by the over-optimistic appraisals of the market that has been made by entrepreneurs. Such rosy glasses have been tinted in part by the artificial activity encouraged by instalment-plan buying.

WHEN STRIKES STRIKE INSTALMENTS

In the past, it has been the experience of finance companies that the amount of repossessions during a period of unemployment has been relatively small. Many of the finance companies have drawn up figures and charts. These are presented to show their actual losses during a prolonged strike. Such losses have not been great even in sections such as the anthracite field, where the greater part of the community's income is represented by miners' wages.

Experience to date, however, does not appear conclusive that, in a period of labor strife, both purchasers on instalments and the community do not suffer economic loss. Delinquencies are prevalent during such emergencies. Often there is an actual moratorium on payments. This condition is dangerous for the same reason that "frozen loans" are bad for a commercial bank. Frozen loans lower the liquidity of the organization that does the underwriting. Although finance companies, unlike a commercial bank, do not have to meet demand obligations, they must be in a position to meet their own maturing loans. Unless they are able to turn over their capital at a normal rate, they naturally face a diminution of profits.

Naturally it is to the interests both of seller and of buyer that the purchaser does not contract beyond his ability to pay. Therefore, as a matter of self interest, it is up to retail merchants and finance companies to dissuade the customer from over-buying. This avoids the dissatisfaction that will result if he does over-extend himself.

FOOLISH BUYS AND UNWISE SALES

A "foolish purchase" by the buyer or an "unwise sale" by the dealer may contribute to an unhealthy credit condition. To avoid such a situation is in the best interests of us all. Therefore, I have come to the conclusion that the only justification for instalment sales is in the case of certain capital goods. I have in mind cases where the buyer can ultimately convert a current expenditure into a fixed asset and increase his net worth.

In the matter of consumers' goods, the line is difficult to draw. Consider automobiles, oil burners, air-conditioning equipment and other relatively high-priced articles. Here the use of the product may contribute to the buyer's health or earning capacity. It may improve his efficiency. From such arguments, buying on a time-payment basis may have some justification.

It is difficult to see any sound basis for encouraging the instalment buying of "soft goods"—clothing, in particular. The buyer of this merchandise probably will never have a large investment,—an important equity which he can be encouraged to protect at some sacrifice. Aside from any deterioration of the moral fiber of the buyer, such undue exploitation of instalment buying will create an unhealthy expansion. It offers temptation to companies which produce to satisfy such a demand. It puts industries in vulnerable positions where they have all the farther to fall when the country again hits a point in the business cycle similar to 1932.

PAPER PROFITS AND INSTALMENT SALES

I have stated that the volume of instalment sales reached a peak in 1929. During 1932 and 1933 the spread between this type of sale and that made for cash or on thirty days' credit increased materially. The explanation probably is two-fold. First, a large part of the consuming public did not have the purchasing power to replace a good many articles that had outlived their usefulness. Second, those who were able to make new purchases in many cases refrained for fear of further salary cuts or the loss of employment.

The stock market "averages" showed sustained recovery throughout 1935 and 1936. The great consumer class was encouraged to borrow against its future income. At the close of 1936, the volume of instalment credit outstanding was stated to have been about 6.4% of total wages and salaries paid during the year.

Probably by mid-1937, or prior to the recession in the stock market which began in August, this figure was between 5% and 6% of total income for the year. As the decline of stock prices became more acute during the closing months of 1937, retail sales (either for cash or credit) fell off quite noticeably.

ROLE OF STOCK MARKETS

In the past the stock market traditionally has been regarded as a barometer for forecasting the near-term business outlook. This indicator hitherto has worked out fairly satisfactorily. Capital has been willing to take a greater or a lesser risk according to the stock-market trend. Labor has felt either liberal or conservative in expending its wages according to the psychological feeling. Sentiment as to business conditions has been closely keyed to the trend of common stock prices.

Prior to the 1920's, the wage earner was inclined to avoid contractual obligations so that he could alter his standard of living according to his income. Capital naturally is not in such a good tactical position to adapt itself quickly to changes in business sentiment. Corporations are somewhat at the mercy of fixed charges entering into the cost of production. These exist despite the appearance given to the profit and loss statement. By pledging a part of his future income the wage earner is allowing himself also to be jockeyed into a pocket. He is put into a position similar to that of the unfortunate entrepreneur who cannot adjust his costs materially by altering his production schedule.

During the recovery phase of each business cycle there have been those who have purchased real estate on the proverbial shoe-string. They have lost title to their property when their incomes became temporarily depleted. They have not had a sufficient reserve to meet their constant costs in the form of taxes, interest, insurance, etc. A fall in real estate values customarily follows deflation of common stock prices. This often wipes out any equity value which the real estate holder may have originally possessed.

Sometimes the purchaser of consumer's goods on a partial-payment basis recognizes that he has an equity. He realizes that it is to his advantage to retain this equity. Without such an attitude there is likely to be a weakness throughout the entire instalment structure. Added to this factor is the item of changing styles for all types of articles. This may result in an article becoming obsolete before the purchaser has met his final payment. An over-extension of instalment sales hastens stock-market collapses; while such collapses greatly increase the losses of consumers.

SALARIED WORKERS IN JEOPARDY

A very dangerous situation exists where we have the salaried worker buying both common stocks on margin and household articles on the instalment plan. Such a situation prevailed during the period of market recovery in 1936-1937. As a member of the *nouveaux riches,* a consumer's old standard of living is felt to be no longer adequate. He hastens to move to a more pretentious home. He purchases more elaborate furnishings. He buys a bigger and better car. He manifests an interest in many luxurious articles concerning which he formerly may have had only an academic knowledge. He is tempted to acquire more of these comforts and conveniences than he can afford. He cherishes the fond hope that his market operations will greatly increase his income. He pictures profits that will enable him to write a check for his luxuries in the near future. Hence he admits no reason to defer his enjoyments, since the coveted goods can be acquired "on the cuff."

With very few exceptions, the people who persist in riding the crest in this way come to grief. They rarely take any profits from their security trading. They are always convinced that the market is going higher. They fail to recognize that at some point the end must come. Then the feeling will develop that the stock market has over-discounted the business outlook. Prices will begin to weaken. Our "financial wizard" friend, operating his margin account, will feel that such a condition is only temporary. It may become necessary for him to put up more margin. He throws in what little money he can scrape together by making additional loans, if possible. He lets the butcher, the baker, and the candlestick maker wait. The final outcome is obvious and sad to contemplate.. Our friend's trading account is sold out. He is severely pressed to meet instalment payments on his newly acquired symbols of prosperity. He becomes bitter against the prevailing social order. Too often he becomes a ruined man.

A REMEDY WORSE THAN THE MALADY?

Instalment credit, no doubt, has for a time facilitated the growth of mass-production industries. It may have contributed something to some price reductions that have followed. We must, however, be very careful how we use this powerful device. Everybody longs to cure dull business. Surely, however, we do not want a remedy worse than the malady. At least we must try to minimize disturbing effects upon the credit structure of the country. An interesting possibility has been suggested. It is to increase the proportion of instalment selling that is financed through investment funds and decrease that proportion which is financed through bank credit. Unless this is done, it will surely be necessary in some way to offset its deflationary effects during a period of debt contraction. This may perhaps again be done by increased Government spending; but only at the expense of property holders for generations to come.

CHAPTER SEVEN

CAN CONSUMERS PROTECT THEMSELVES?

*"A man in debt is caught in a net; yes, loans and
debts make worries and frets."—John Ray*

Students of history will recall the case of a cértain
kind-hearted man. He was humane, sensitive, averse
to inflicting pain. When faced with the necessity of
cutting off his dog's tail—in order to "ease" the ani-
mal's suffering—he cut off the tail only an inch at a
time. On a par with this perverted reasoning is the
theory of "easy" payment plans. The original pro-
totype of such contracts was the tail-cutting scheme
mentioned above. Promoters of instalment buying
have ransacked the dictionaries to find fair words to
describe a system that can become essentially unfair
to the consumer and destructive to the merchant.
Advertising writers have toiled far into the night to
connect the partial-payment business with the respectability of "Credit." Many a family which would shrink
from smirching itself with any mere Dollar-Down-
And-Dime-A-Day stuff saves its face with a comforting idea: Instalment buying is glossed with the dignity
of "consumption credit." This euphemism of "credit"
suggests to the gullible that part-payment plans are
akin to the practices of the great corporations, or even
the Government itself!

Another word which is hallowed by associations with the good, the true and the beautiful, is "Budget." Therefore some of the publicity artists have not hesitated to sprinkle their instalment traps with the perfume of "budgeting," "planning," and even—spare their souls—"thrift"! The very fact of this anxious search to find ways to sugar-coat the nasty pill reveals that instalment buying, as occasionally practised, may be replete with evils. Reviewing some of the ways in which this game, when run by unscrupulous operators, bedevils the consumer, we find a shocking tale of grief.

Much of the merchandise itself is rumored to be specially manufactured for this trade, and may be shoddily built, grossly under-valued, rankly over-priced. Sometimes the article can hardly be called a bargain even if the down payment alone were the only price and no further contributions were ever collected. When stripped of ingenious quirks and seen in stark reality, the rate of interest—usury—exacted from the hapless buyer by some heartless operators is undeniably rapacious. Furthermore, when any method of merchandising becomes corrupted it has a baleful effect upon sound retailing. The tendency of the reckless type of instalment selling is to lift prices, depress standards, and corrupt trade. Thus instalment vices are sure to damage not only its direct victims, but all the public as well, including other retailers and the better class of instalment operators.

ADDICTS ACQUIRE AN "INSTAL-MENTALITY"

We used the word "instal-mentality" to describe the mental attitude acquired by the addict of instalment buying when marked by vicious excesses. Observation of case histories shows that the deterioration is far-reaching. The inroads of the instalment attack by the unethical promoter are not only pecuniary but spiritual. In the end, pocketbook, bank-account, and character, all degenerate where the business is mismanaged. Therefore the problem expands in scope. Here is more than a stray instance of some silly working-girl who was enticed into buying a fur coat beyond her means. Here is more than a chance mishap of some family which snarled itself in a contract, not with responsible finance companies but with tricksters, and bound itself for poor furniture at extortionate prices and ruinous rates of interest.

Some of the perversions of the instalment epidemic have gone far beyond a few isolated and insignificant incidents. The trouble has swollen to the dimensions of a full-scale social "situation." This is because of the reactions from indulgence in this habit-forming narcotic prepared in poisonous forms and peddled by the irresponsible. Such practices corrode and break down the character, distorting the views and conduct in all the relations of life. Such spoilage is infectious. The sweep of the injudicious debt habit and philosophy invades the innocent along with the guilty.

Therefore arises the question how consumers can protect themselves from the bombing by this enemy, this outlaw who knows no limit to his mispractices. Of the many safeguards which consumers can erect for their protection, none will avail unless consumers first develop sounder character. An enemy such as those who depart from standards set by sound finance companies always searches out the weak spots. Biologists when attacking a pest look first for the vulnerable stages in the insect's life cycle. Military attack aims where the column or front is thin.

Consumers are weak in their false pride which tempts into extravagances. They seek not chiefly intrinsic enjoyment, but to "keep up" with the lavishness of friends and neighbors. In this respect, the pace-setting Joneses have done villainous damage. Consumers are weak in patience, with childish inability to await possession in God's good time. They are weak in the pioneer virtues of industry, sacrifice, and thrift. They are weak in knowledge of values and appraisal of prices. All this is weakness of character. Only an inner strengthening here can give full and lasting protection against instalment perils.

SAFEGUARDS BY CONSUMER EDUCATION

Protection against the dangers of a vicious use of the instalment plans was one of my purposes in establishing Buyers Business Schools. I want now to tell you briefly the story of this adventure in education. At the start I placed these schools in various representative cities throughout New England. This local network gave me typical cross-sections of the consuming public. At the same time the territory was compact enough for efficient experiment and supervision. In each of the selected cities I secured suitable buildings, engaged an instructing corps and arranged for a staff of visiting lecturers. The course covers a period of thirty-five weeks, five school-days a week. Part of this schedule is allotted to visits to nearby factories, stores, and other business establishments. At the start, the sessions were held during the day and were intended only for full-time students. I soon discovered, however, there was a demand for evening courses for those who could not spare the time during the day. Accordingly I added a night school for those who want to get their training outside of their regular activities. Housewives or others may attend single lectures on subjects in which they are specially interested.

Such a school can teach consumers how to protect themselves against the iniquities of instalments when not operated by upright companies. It can train people in sound and wholesome ways to provide for their consumption needs. Such positive education is one of the surest safeguards against the encroachment of destructive and debasing methods. A typical school week, for example, includes the intensive study of some one household commodity such as fuel, linens, or rugs. This merchandise training is supported by instruction in buying-fundamentals, such as: accounting, budget-making, nation-wide and local marketing. Although these broader subjects provide an invaluable background, they are not permitted to usurp the specialized attention to specific goods and services. How to buy this commodity or that—a different one each week—these real problems of real buyers stand out in the school program.

Early in the school year, students are warned of the pits which unscrupulous manufacturers or merchants can dig to catch the unwary. This course in buymanship is intended to turn the flood-lights full upon the dark places, the rotten floorboards and broken stairs of merchandise distribution. Particularly emphasized are the fallacies of instalment contracts as twisted by undesirable practitioners. I am convinced that such an eye-opener deserves a place near the start of any purchasing study. Students should be constantly coached in this fundamental: The most favorable purchasing terms necessarily are always obtainable by paying cash. In contrast, instalment credit puts the seller in the driver's seat, makes him the man-on-horseback, and puts the buyer under the whip and rowel. Classes will learn by repeated illustrations that there is only one really *"easy* payment"—and that is cash on the nail.

At the same time, in the midst of all this "laboratory" work, I try never to lose sight of this truth: The only conclusive protection of consumers will come, not merely from imparting instruction, but from the simultaneous strengthening of character. That is what puts genuine armor upon consumers, guarding them against all attacks. For that reason all consumer schools labor to improve students' health and personal habits, and to acquaint them with the elements of biology, psychology, and dietary laws. Students soon come to appreciate the ignorance, carelessness, and extravagance of instalment buying on ill-advised contracts. This is contrasted with the efficiency and economy of scientific purchasing.

Ability to pay cash for goods and services is a bedrock necessity for the most proficient buying. The fact that many merchants and families fail to do this is one reason why jobbers and retailers are obliged to charge such high prices. To secure goods at lower prices—or goods of higher quality at the same prices—consumers must help reduce the selling costs of those from whom they buy. The instalment system, in its misapplications, increases selling costs. These thoughts are typical of some of the truths our schools endeavor to teach. When consumers know the truth, they will be better equipped to free themselves from the shackles of degrading debt. They can shuck off the fetters imposed by concerns which are a disgrace to the honest membership of the industry they represent.

BARE-SPOTS IN AMERICAN EDUCATION

Educational institutions of every grade, from secondary to collegiate, are beginning to include such courses as domestic economics. The public is awaking to the fact that men and women spend but a fraction of their lives in the activities of *producing*. The activities of *consuming* are the side of life in which mankind finds final expression. Educators have over-emphasized the money-earning functions and have under-emphasized the money-spending functions. The schools have taught how to *write* advertising. They have not taught adequately how to *read* advertising—how to read it with liberal discounting of claims and healthy skepticism of promises. They have trained their students in sales promotion but have neglected to give instruction in the equally vital arts of sales *resistance*.

The above situation gradually is being corrected. The introduction of courses in domestic science has broken the ice. It has prepared for some real progress in educating our young people in Buymanship. Already one obstacle has intruded. There is a natural temptation among manufacturers and merchants to flood the teachers with "instruction material" descriptive of merchandise. Of course such descriptions, exhibits and samples, are propaganda. Teachers will be an easy prey to such campaigns until the teachers themselves have the energy to develop their own factual data, prepared in the sole interests of the consumer.

Few of the domestic science courses in colleges and secondary schools adequately teach the danger and damage of instalment buying. This is why we say that there is a bare-spot in the American education system. Admittedly it is a topic which would arouse instantly a storm of controversy if introduced into the school courses. If any teacher in a public school or college should attempt to expound the evils of the instalment business as practiced by local merchants, you can picture the reactions. Such a teacher would be subjected to relentless pressure from countless sources, and to a ruthless ousting campaign. Academic freedom does not yet exist—not this degree of freedom. Will our teachers ever be in a position to exercise the independence and courage to tell the truth about the misapplications of instalment buying?

INSTALMENT *saving* VS. INSTALMENT *buying*

Thus far, then, we have answered in three ways the question: how can consumers protect themselves against injuries from injudicious instalment-plan propaganda and pressure? The *first* method is the fundamental upbuilding of character. Harsh realism compels us to admit that the victims of "instalmentality" are recruited chiefly from the ranks of the defectives in character. The *second* method of protection is through special schools devoted exclusively to the training of consumers. The *third* method is through courses of domestic science and similar subjects in our general colleges and secondary schools. Let them dare to disclose the real facts about the viciousness of instalment schemes as practised by crafty manipulators.

We now turn to a further safeguard of the public. This we will describe as a counter-attack. It is fighting fire with fire. It is the further development of instalment *saving*. This first began, on a big scale, with the Christmas Club idea. The banks during the year received from their depositors who joined the club, periodic deposits. These were accumulated; and just before Christmas the total was paid as a lump sum, convenient for holiday purchasing. As I will later suggest, this club idea has great possibilities for development.

About ten years ago I published a Special Letter, under the title "Instalment Saving." The message in that letter was substantially as follows. There is nothing wrong with the instalment idea *per se*, provided it is applied to saving rather than spending. People will do things by instalments that they will not do in a lump. Unless we can find a safe and sound way to utilize instalment psychology, we must be reconciled to the fact that some customers will rarely buy anything that costs over $50 or $100. If all dealers were suddenly to insist upon cash alone, without any other help, some of the big industries of the countries might seriously be crippled by the stoppage of orders. Overlooking their potential vices, instalment plans undeniably have enlarged the scope of consumer demand. From a sheer economic standpoint, it makes little difference whether people buy large units or small, or whether they buy refrigerators or tennis rackets. However, it makes a radical and fundamental difference whether people pay cash for the goods or run into debt.

"CLUB" SAVING HAS POSSIBILITIES

We have been through enough swings of the business pendulum to see what happens to the debtor when general conditions dash him on the rocks. The moment an individual puts himself in debt, he forfeits automatically his claims to independence. He signs up as the servant of the lender. Before he gets through with it, he may pay dearly for serving. When a whole nation of consumers gets into unjustifiable debt, a very unhealthy condition prevails and all business suffers therefrom. Because some ill-advised instalment propaganda has imparted to debt a false air of respectability, it in no wise alters the economic perils. No wiles of advertising can make wholesome and sound what is inherently perilous. On the one hand, therefore, is the urgent clamor for business among the great industries to which instalment buying has given an enlarged outlet. On the other hand, there is the yawning pitfall of excessive debt. There is one way out. It has been demonstrated by the practical success of such plans as the Christmas Club. Here is an idea which should be extended to many more fields. Here is a way in which consumers can protect themselves against the barb-wire entanglements of instalment buying. I have previously touched upon this subject; but its fundamental importance calls for further elaboration.

These original clubs frequently have run up year-end savings into hundreds of millions of dollars. A billion dollar annual total should easily be maintained in this one section of our economy alone. The principle, however, ought to be extended in many other directions. The plan inculcates the habits of systematic saving. Such funds are accumulated all through the year. The consumer makes his payments in convenient amounts at intervals corresponding to the time that the average individual receives his wages or salary. The club depositors use the instalment principle, but with two distinct differences. (1) Instead of *paying* interest on their money, they *receive* interest. (2) Instead of buying at top prices, they can go into the stores with cash in hand and get the benefit of every bargain offered. Nothing talks in such a loud and commanding voice as cash. We estimate that such buyers can get from 10% to 15% more value for their money than do the victims of unwise instalment contracts.

WHY PAY HIGHER PRICES?

Thus the club member who practices instalment *saving* has a handsome gain over the slave of instalment *buying*. The slogan of the consumer should be: "Those who have the sense to walk while they pay, may soon ride at a reduced price." If sufficiently developed, the simple and effective Christmas-club plan has tremendous possibilities for securing better merchandise for less money. There is no real reason why the fundamental principles of such a club should be limited to a single occasion and season. Consumers could protect themselves by forming, for example, an automobile savings club. This could mature in the spring when many people schedule their purchase of cars. Already there have been some vacation clubs operated, with the year maturing in July or August. There could be a going-away-winters club; a seasonal clothing club; a children's college-education club; and a coal or oil club. This is a way to club unworthy instalment contractors into either retreat or reform!

Most of the goods and services which are now bought on instalments might be bought to better advantage by these savings-club plans. Some economists have estimated this program would increase the total volume of business and the amount of earnings for the legitimate manufacturer, dealer, and banker. Remember the inner trait of human nature to want to do things on instalments. This natural instinct should be capitalized for the welfare of consumers—not exploited to their injury. Those deficient in fairness both to their customers and to reputable finance companies deserve no consideration. It would· be an immeasurable public service to help people to do their *saving* with instalments, and their *spending* with cash. This would increase permanently the total amount of business. Surely it would put business in a more stable position and establish it upon a sounder basis. It may well be that the final solution of this whole instalment-plan problem will be found not in killing the instalment idea, but in utilizing it to build up customers by teaching them to save in advance.

FRIENDS OF YOUR FAMILY

According to analysis, the weeds of instalment plans flourish and choke legitimate business, because of two chief reasons. In the first place, the consumer himself has soft shoulders and yields to the coaxing, wheedling, skullduggery, and bulldozing of the instalment sharks. In the second place, our general business system has grave faults of mechanism; periodically it gets out of smooth adjustment. Every decade the maladjustments accumulate so mightily that consumers do not get enough income to take away the products of industry at prices which permit industrial earnings. It is not the socialists' theory that the profit system of business is mathematically impossible continuously. Rather it is a realistic facing of the historic fact that every once in a while business requires adjustment and tuning up like any other complex machinery operated by careless and clumsy human beings. Now these two factors, the frailty of both humans and economic mechanisms, conspire to create a terrific pressure to expand instalment buying. Hundreds of the most powerful influences are driving the average family to slip into debt.

Are there counter-forces operating on the other side, struggling to help the average family to keep out of debt and at the same time provide adequate standards of living? Yes, there are such friends of your family. Their number is growing. Among the friendly influences we count those organizations which make a specialty of investigating merchandise and reporting upon the relative merits and values of competing goods. We welcome also the work of a few officials and Congressmen in Federal service, together with some genuine statesmen of the states. These crusaders are striving for governmental help to consumers in the fight to protect themselves from raids by the instalmenteers—those who would pervert a legitimate institution. Assuredly the excesses of the instalment business should be curbed by more rigorous legislation on down payments, duration of contracts, class of merchandise, rates, and truthful dealings. Such laws should be supplemented by severe and ceaseless regulation by officials who will serve the public first.

IN UNION CONSUMERS FIND STRENGTH

Instalment business has become big business. In the main it is in the hands of sound and responsible managers. There has developed, however, an objectionable stratum. The undesirable are too resourceful, resolute and well-entrenched for an individual family to resist or combat. Such a conflict is pitifully one-sided. Therefore, we look to the merging of individual families into associations which can meet organized exploitation with organized protection. Many such unions of consumers already exist. Where such associations are honestly operated in the sole interests of consumers and enjoy able leadership, we are prepared to extend to them our heartiest approbation and support. Our criticism of their programs and platforms, however, refers to the failure to attack the excesses of instalment buying as violently as they should. Wholly as a constructive suggestion, we offer to bona fide organizations of consumers the recommendation that they put on a vigorous campaign against instalment abuses. If our study of this situation has revealed any one thing, it is this. No campaign of self-help for persecuted consumers is likely to accomplish much if it confines its efforts to purely negative measures. You can hope for success largely in proportion to your emphasis on acceptable substitutes.

I hope to see consumers' organizations strengthen their position in Washington. If driven to such necessity, let lobbies be met with lobbies as fire is fought by fire. The job of keeping the clamps on instalment contracting would be an excellent project for a Federal Department for the Consumer. If anybody protests that such restriction and regulation is going too far and putting the Government into paternalism, I can only retort that many an instalment devotee certainly needs a papa. The action of some families in signing up unfavorable instalment contracts convicts them of credulity, gullibility, and asininity. The courts ought to appoint a guardian for such folks!

CONSUMERS' COÖPERATIVE PROTECTION

In many ways the most promising agency whereby purchasers can protect themselves against being drawn into a tanglefoot of debt is the public's own organization. This is the growing network of Consumers' Coöperative Societies, now reaching into all three divisions of Retailing, Wholesaling, and Producing. This modern development of a time-honored institution is a most significant economic movement. It is worthy of note that wherever consumers' coöperation is thriving and expanding it is built four-square on the foundation of cash payments—with a strict taboo on debt. The pioneers of coöperation were not searching for the easiest way. Their goal was the soundest, most secure and lasting way of increasing the consumer's real buying power and furthering his permanent prosperity. These hard-headed and clear-eyed leaders would have kicked aside in disgust the Fool's Gold of the perverted type of part payments. They sought reality. These Consumers' Coöperative Societies refused to build on the quicksand of misapplied instalment plans. They built on the enduring rock of cash.

Another feature which the successful coöperatives have emphasized is education. They insist upon the continuous practical training of their members in the principles and practices of household and personal buying. Most of the societies bind themselves in their articles of organization to appropriate annually a stipulated percentage of their revenues for such education purposes. With sincere admiration for what these societies are accomplishing, I suggest that they make even more aggressive efforts to educate their members against the devastation of instalment buying when it falls into the clutches of anti-social operators. It is true that their members cannot buy on instalments at the societies' stores. They are subjected, however, to the allurements of outside corrupters. Moreover, non-members have confidence in the society's teachings, for its success is widely known. Warning against the termites of instalment should be notably effective coming from authorities who are held in such high regard. Such coöperation in battling the evils of instalments would most effectively reinforce the line-up on the side of consumers.

INFLATION—NEW MENACE TO INSTALMENT PRISONERS

It is well worth our while to demolish one of the most insidious fallacies among the many false doctrines used to powder the sores of the instalment delusion.   I refer again to the fallacious idea that drastic inflation does not engulf instalment prisoners and other debtors.   It is plausible to expect that the first wavelets of an inflation tide will wash gently on the feet of the debtor.   A symptom of inflation is rising prices of goods and services with advancing costs of living.   Therefore, if you had contracted for instalment merchandise and taken the goods into your own hands, would you not favorably be situated in a day of mounting prices?   Again, a symptom of inflation is the rotting of the currency.   If you can make your instalment payments in "phony" money after getting a price on the basis of good money would not this give you the drop on your creditors?   Superficial arguments of this kind have always been used by debtors and prospective debtors to delude themselves into a fool's dream of inflation.   Under such distorted reasoning inflation is visioned as something which can transmute liabilities into assets, expense into income, and folly into wisdom.   Hail inflation! O debt, where is thy sting?   O instalment shark, thy victory?

The trouble with that utopia of the would-be debtor, as I have previously indicated, is that it does not work out that way.   Speedily, sometimes with an explosive suddenness that takes even the shrewdest speculator unaware, the wavelets of inflation mount into a raging flood. Or, to reverse the figure, inflation can be compared better to a conflagration: A tiny spark may kindle a prairie fire that consumes everything in its path. The experience of other countries which have succumbed to drastic inflation shows that it may overcome and ruin even the most nimble, resourceful and audacious. If that is so, and history abundantly proves the statement, then what ghost of a chance has the luckless debtor? He is weighted down by his chains of unwise instalment contracts in the mad tumult of an inflation stampede and mania. Any weakminded and shallow optimist who hopes to stick his head into the jaws of debt and trust to inflation to pull him out, is doomed. When threatened with any extreme of currency gyration, whether inflation or deflation, do not rush into debt. Rather, get out of debt!

IF WORSE COMES TO WORST

I can readily foresee a possibility that the day may come when the misapplication of instalment buying may result in a crisis of major degree. My reasons for this foreboding are as follows: Periodically this country—in common with many other nations—has been caught in the toils of the business cycle. We have been laid low with a famine of purchasing power, gripping the nation in a so-called depression. Failure of purchasing power catches all classes in desperate plight. Industrial workers, together with the chronically under-privileged, are in dire need of the rudiments of food, shelter, and clothing. Manufacturers are desperate for orders; merchants for sales. Farmers simultaneously are in lack of merchandise and markets. Bankers are in want for safe and profitable opportunities to make loans. Investors suffer deprivation of dividend checks on their stocks, or even interest payments on their bonds. In agonizing straits which are caused by dearth of purchasing power all groups are tempted to take the broad and easy path that leads to destruction. They are lured by the enticements of those who offer the instalment stimulus as a sure cure for the deficiency of purchasing power.

It takes little imagination to picture a scene of this kind, when common sense crumbles and the population rushes up the beckoning heights of an instalment boom. Such a craze could end only at a precipice, with a sheer drop straight into economic chaos. Faced with the possibility of such catastrophe—and it is well within the bounds of realism—it is only ordinary prudence to lay our plans of procedure. Just as the pupils of a school are trained in a fire-drill to avert disaster in event of emergency, our people should be drilled against economic crises. In case of an emergency, due either to instalment excesses or other perils, the first step is to set aside group hostilities and unite in coöperative action. Therefore, in the unhappy event that an instalment craze ever puts this nation into extreme peril, let us be ready. Let us be prepared to turn in a swift and orderly manner to the supreme cure for any crisis, namely: A coalition government to have and hold power for the duration of the emergency.

CHALLENGE TO THE INDUSTRY

Always it is a mistake to paint any reputable industry as a nest of rascals just because of the misbehavior of a few miscreants. I picture, and sincerely so, the responsible leaders of the instalment business as just as honest, as high-minded, and as whole-heartedly devoted to the public welfare, as the directors of any other great industry. Many of these men I count as lifetime friends and acquaintances. In their place I probably would be compelled to do as they are doing. Instead of reproaching me for my criticisms and instead of merely standing on the defensive, it is my hope, therefore, that the real leaders of the business will join with me on the consumers' front.

Help me show a bewildered and hard-pressed people how consumers can protect themselves against abuses of the instalment system! It is shortsighted policy for any man of integrity in instalment plans to condone and harbor the malpractitioners in that industry. When they act as apologists for wrong doers, the leaders are but conniving at their own downfall. Therefore instead of berating a constructive critic, let the sound representatives of the instalment industry use their energies to start a purge of the racketeers. That has been my creed in writing this book, and one of the reasons why I have felt free to attack without pulling my punches.

HIDDEN INSTALMENTS YOU PAY

Probably about half the people who read the fore-going advice on how consumers can protect themselves against instalment evils, may say to themselves:

"That is all right for other folks, but our family is different. We do not need safeguards, because we never would think of doing such a thing as buying on instalments. Let Babson talk to the poor, deluded, deadbeats who have not brains to keep away from this dangerous and costly game."

Hence a word to the wise,—those who never in all their lives signed an instalment contract, and there-fore imagine they are not paying tribute to the in-stalment business. To open the eyes of these pious and complacent people let me tell this true story. In Florida, where I spend my winters, one day I was making a tour of inspection of a certain district. In my rambles I came upon a new refreshment stand which had just been opened. I noticed a very fine mechanical refrigerator to hold various flavors of ice cream. Being somewhat interested in the mechanical refrigeration industry, I asked the manager of the re-freshment stand what his refrigerator cost. To my astonishment, he replied:

"I do not know what it cost. It came crated from the factory, a perfectly new machine; the concern from which we buy our ice cream supplies the re-frigerator without charge."

That aroused my curiosity. I next hunted up the concern which supplies this ice cream. I asked the manager how he could afford to provide a customer free of charge with a new refrigerator costing several hundred dollars. He answered:

"That's easy. I buy it from the manufacturer on the instalment plan, with a small payment each month. I add the amount of this monthly payment—and a little more—to the price of the ice cream. I find this is one of the best ways to sell ice cream,—and in the end the scheme costs me nothing."

Moral: *Even when you and I buy a plate of ice cream for cash, we're still in danger of being gypped by some insidious instalment racket.*

Confess that when you have entered some handsome store, whatever the size or the line of business, that has beautiful, fresh appointments and every imaginable equipment, you have been impressed. You have jumped to the conclusion: Here is prosperity and success, here is an excellent establishment with which to deal. Wait a moment, however! How much of that lavish layout is the real property of the store? How much belongs actually to some manufacturer or finance company? The old saying was "fine feathers do not make a fine bird." Nowadays we must be even more cynical: The fine feathers may not even *belong* to the bird, but may be *instalment* feathers!

Who pays for the sumptuous and regal luxury of some of our modern palaces of trade? Who in the end foots the bills in the form of padded prices and overcharges which are necessitated to meet instalment expenses? The consumer pays, as always. Let no family fool itself with the comforting delusion that merely laying down cash money on the counter will assure a customer of the benefits that rightly belong to him who buys for cash. That may have been partly true once. It is not at all true today. Therefore before you go into ecstasies over the glories of your dealer's place of business, look twice and think thrice. Is some manufacturer or finance company exacting from you an extra price for these alluring appurte- nances? How many articles for which you pay cash (and thereby are entitled to the benefit of bottom prices) are loaded with super-charges—charges added to the price, with a little more? The finance com- panies are not running their enterprise as a hobby. They are not pleased merely to meet expenses and operate at cost. They expect earnings, profits. Are you glad to pay such profits in the form of boosted prices?

The next time you are trading at a pretentious mod- ern store, give the premises a cold-blooded scrutiny. Observe the "store-front," gleaming with the latest discoveries of the glass, metal, and plastic industries. Inside, study the counters and showcases, the shelves and merchandise display devices, or the refrigeration and other equipment. Perhaps you can estimate in a rough way what some of this installation costs; then tack on some profits for instalment financing; finally, pile the whole percentage burden on the prices you are required to pay. Perhaps you are willing to pay the price plus. On the other hand, after figuring costs, you may decide to walk out.

WHAT WAY OUT?

If you object to carrying the load of hidden instalment payments at a certain store, where shall you go for your goods? That is not so simple. Already I have outlined some of the sources and channels whereby desperate consumers are seeking protection from the regimentation and dictatorship of instalmenteers. As a final suggestion, I wish to commend various groups which are helping consumers to buy more goods for their money. Specifically I have in mind some of the so-called merchandise service organizations. I expect to see such organizations spring up in increasing numbers and scope of operations. They are a response to the people's cry for help and its demand to buy in the lowest priced legitimate markets.

For instance, it has been estimated that sometimes a manufacturer may get not much over $40 for a piece of furniture on which some retail store may set a price of perhaps $100. If that manufacturer sells through jobbers, then the price may be a little more. Let us assume that represents approximately the situation and the furniture is to be shipped directly from the factory.

Now comes the service organization. It may require that you go to some back street and climb some stairs. Nevertheless, you should be willing to go to this extra trouble if after the organization takes 20% for its charge, you get the desired piece of furniture for around $65 cash. Do not misinterpret my position. I am not condemning a mark-up of 100% in criticism of the conventional retailers. I grant that mark-ups in this range are probably needed by retailers who must do business along methods which ninety per cent of their customers demand. Such methods require expensive locations, elaborate stocks, expert attention, long credits and return privileges. Retailers—on the other hand—should in turn not resent the distribution work of these service groups. They supply a real need. They take care of those few consumers who are willing to pay cash, forego stylish streets, climb stairs, and go to considerable inconvenience—perhaps waiting for merchandise to come from the factory. The money which these energetic customers thus save can be spent by them in department and other stores to buy goods which otherwise they would be unable to afford. This not only raises the standard of living for the clients of these service organizations, but increases employment for the nation as a whole.

FUTURE OF RETAIL TRADE

There is a place for all forms of merchandising: house-to-house canvassing, department stores, mail-order houses, specialty shops, chain stores, super-markets and perhaps other developments in the future. Service organizations are simply one more new form of distribution designed for consumers who have patience in filling their real needs, but no patience in submitting to excess prices for extravagant facilities. Incidentally, readers may be interested in the fact that the experimental Buyers Schools, to which I have already referred, are undertaking to train agents for merchandise service organizations. In this connection I am developing a "laboratory" to test what specific savings can be made by families willing to pay cash and go to some additional trouble in their household shopping. Any progress which can be made along this line ought to be of interest to everybody, including the traditional retail establishments. Occasionally some retail or trade association which is not yet awake to social trends, may protest such study and research. They may even threaten to stir up their jobbers to hostility against our educational work and the activities of the service groups. That would be the same kind of mistake which wage workers make when smashing or sabotaging modern labor-saving machinery. "Business makes business" is true in all fields. Protection of consumers against exploitation builds up customers. It enlarges trade opportunities for merchandising in all its legitimate branches.

As a final word on this subject of protecting consumers: Be prepared to work for MASS-CONSUMPTION whenever the opportunity develops in your community. Mass-consumption, as fathered by Frederick Purdy of 342 Madison Avenue, New York City, brings forward individual planning as the alternative to national planning. In this it is new. This country is not ready for national planning. It may never be ready. But every day brings evidence that there is a great reaching out by the people for advancement through coöperation; and to this we believe mass-consumption provides an answer. National planning inevitably leads to fascism. Individual action strengthens the fibers of democracy.

Under the principles of mass-consumption, consumers would budget their incomes and make known through a central office the goods they intend to buy. Their total requirements would set the rate of industrial output. Producers would bid competitively on these proposed purchases. Goods could be shipped direct to consumers. The elements in mass-consumption, through which the small producer is afforded the same business advantages as the 'larger one, are of promise. It is fortunate if the vitality of small business may be sustained. It is well to have a diffusion of influences, whether or not intentionally menacing, with which the country may have to contend.

Mass-consumption is not to be mistaken as following the consumer-coöperative idea. Its economies are above and beyond the coöperative technic, for it avoids stores and wholesaling. Resourceful distributors, however, should meet the challenge with new contributions to merchandising efficiency. Mass-consumption gets productive activity under way without first calling for money-spending by people who do not have money to spend. It brings into coördination the productive abilities and the needs of the unemployed and the impecunious to establish them in employment and security. It makes effective the economies and efficiencies of our present system of mass-production. Mass-consumption points a way toward the ending of business cycles and depressions.

CHAPTER EIGHT

WHAT NOT TO BUY ON INSTALMENTS

"Never spend your money before you have it."
—*Thomas Jefferson*

I recall a conversation which I once had with a clear-headed somewhat cynical observer of the business scene. He is a business man himself. He could speak from the depths of personal experience, from *bookkeeping* as well as from *books*. In talking with me, he had taken the rather drastic position that *no* product should *ever* be bought on instalments. I remonstrated with him for such a rabid attitude. I asked him: "Are there not at least a *few* classes of merchandise for which part-payment plans are permissible?" He reflected for a moment in gloomy silence. Then he replied:

"You are right. I think of *one* product for which I make an exception. In fact, I myself would be perfectly willing to buy this product on instalments. It is the casket for my own funeral."

I am sadly aware that the title of this chapter involves an inconsistency. If the main message of the book is the folly of buying on instalments, then it is inconsistent to imply that some products *can* and other products *can not* wisely be thus bought. My predica-

134

ment is: there is little hope of persuading the public to make a right-about-face and put *all* their purchases on a strictly cash basis. That is an ideal beyond reason. The only practical goal is to educate people step by step to pay cash for more and more of their needs. If we cannot aspire to convert erring consumers overnight and make them teetotalers, perhaps we can at least wean them by instalments away from their cups and induce them to taper off the drink habit. Hence I shall force myself to recognize classifications and gradations of merchandise; mentioning some of these groups of products in connection with which the hazards of part payments tend to be minimized. On other descriptions of goods instalment evils are intensified and are seen at their worst. On these latter types of products, partial payments deserve sweeping condemnation; such goods flatly should *not* be bought on instalment. In this chapter I shall gather up some threads of previous discussions and undertake a systematic summary.

First comes the question of *timing* your instalment purchases. At certain stages in the business cycle, instalment buying—although always a contingent danger—tends to offer relatively less risk than at other times. This does not necessarily mean that it is any less costly, extravagant, and objectionable; but merely that the factor of positive peril is less pronounced. For illustration, around the lower reaches of depression, various groups of people face the encouraging probability of gradual recovery of earning power. They enjoy at least a gambling chance that their incomes may gradually increase; or at least that the worst is over. Likewise at that time there is the probability that commodity prices will turn around and begin an upward trend. Therefore in periods such as these a commitment in an instalment contract offers a lower than normal factor of risk.

The danger zone for buying on instalments is during an over-expansion period of the business cycle. At such a stage of fundamental conditions, the family which ties around its neck the millstone of an instalment commitment is inviting pecuniary suicide. Such times create multiple hazards. For instance the breadwinners of the family may lose their jobs in the inevitable crash which follows an abnormal boom. Even if the job is not swept downstream, there is the threatened cut in wage rates, fewer hours, share-the-work drives, and other punishments of depression. Statistics show that health and poise are usually strained by the uncertainties, fears, and sacrifices of a depression. Hard times spare nobody, even although their impact varies with financial circumstances. All families feel the shock in some degree. No family in the clutch of depression is in shape to meet buoyantly the exactions of burdensome instalment contracts with the same light-hearted irresponsibility that marked the assumption of those burdens. It is the disastrous psychology of the instalment system when unscrupulously conducted that its dupes are plastered with their obligations in days of speculative frenzy, and then are

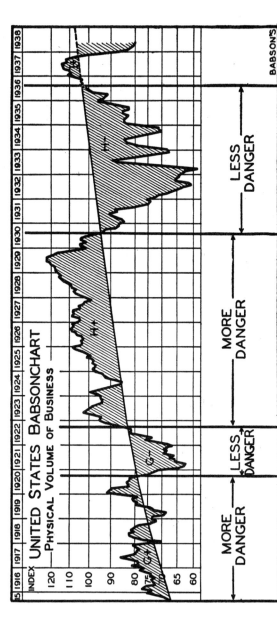

HIGH TIDES AND LOW TIDES OF INSTALMENT DANGER

Representing the nation's commercial and industrial *real* income or progress (in terms of goods and services rather than money). Areas above the diagonal or "normal line" of growth show periods of over-expansion; depressed areas show periods of readjustment.

given the thumb-screws and rack in days of pauperism.

Hence this guiding precept can be laid down. When a business and speculative boom is raging, be careful how you stick your neck into the instalment noose. Applying the same basic principle, resolve to watch your step on instalment commitments in a period when volume of business is above its line of normal growth. In other words, stick to cash purchases when the country is in a period of prosperity. If you *must* buy on instalments, enter into such contracts only when business is below its line of normal growth and the country is chastened by the pangs of depression. Even in a period of hard times, preferably schedule your assumption of debt around the lower levels of business activity. Go slowly after business has once started upon its upward swing into recovery. Many critics doubtless will object that I have set unduly strict standards for indulgence in instalment buying. In answer I reply that the casualty records of business depressions during the past thirty years or more amply support the wisdom of an extremely conservative policy.

SHOULD BUSINESS MEN BUY ON INSTALMENTS?

Inexperienced and untrained consumers perhaps can be forgiven for their follies under the assault of high-pressure instalment merchandising. What shall we say however when hardboiled business men also succumb? Surely, no business concern worthy of the name should be trapped into what William Trufant

Foster amusingly has called "painless debt-istry." Let us reflect upon what should not be bought by business men on the instalment basis. In this way we may be able to develop some principles which will serve as a guide in studying the problem of what the private family should *not* buy by part payments.

Observe that in the early days instalment selling as we know it to our sorrow today, was unknown. No man then dreamed of this coming scourge. The old-fashioned financiers of that day, however frenzied they may have seemed to their own generation, would have thrown up their hands in horror. They would have fainted at the thought of delivering goods to weaklings merely on the down payment of from 20% to 35% of the sales price. They would have been aghast at the proposal that the seller should wait a year or two years before final clean-up of the transaction. Yet today such preposterous terms are becoming the rule rather than the exception in large sections of trade. There are too many operators making a game of the instalment business. They violate the codes and standards recognized by the leaders of this industry.

Not only the naïve and unsophisticated consumer, but even the veteran businessman is being cajoled to buy on instalments all kinds of things. These vary from goods of enduring value and productive utility, to goods representing the acme of quick deterioration and doubtful usefulness. Thus the whole sweep of instalment buying is being carried to extremes, involving customers both among household consumers and commercial enterprisers. These excesses, when viewed against a sane economic background can be described only as a financial phantasy with a very real peril. This is especially true in advance of the inevitable periods of recession and depression. The present absurd lengths to which instalment buying has been pushed are not fully realized. The public is still thinking of part-payment plans in terms of the good old days when even the high-pressure salesman had a heart.

EARLY STANDARDS TOSSED OVERBOARD

What has become of the original idea that the characteristic of instalment merchandise is a high unit price tag? That refers to such things as an automobile truck, store fixtures, and the like. What has happened to the good old ban on long maturities of contract? It looks as if all restrictions were lifted and that the instalment business had plunged outside the pale of law, order, and social safety. Maybe it is only human nature! When sales meet stiff resistance, merchandisers seek new ways to get business. Perhaps if the instalment trend had been handled soundly when it first started, it could have been developed into something non-explosive and non-inflammable at least. Such contracting has been abused instead of decently used. Common sense and reasonable caution in too many instances have long since ceased to prevail. These sales schemes are being exploited altogether too far, particularly in respect to laxness in the types of goods which are being sold in this way.

To be specific, let us review some of the items which

plainly should not be sold on a part-payment basis. Generally speaking it is not objectionable that most types of machinery should be merchandised on instalments, with due observance of conservative financial standards. Nevertheless even in this restricted field there are some notable exceptions. It is questionable whether the instalment plan can properly be applied to the purchase of machinery to be used in new enterprises which are in the experimental stage. A raw and unseasoned promotion or stock-jobbing venture is hardly a fit subject for this type of credit. Another doubtful case arises in connection with the purchase of machinery which is mainly "custom built," or "to order," or highly specialized. This hazard increases if the enterprise is one in which technical changes come swiftly with revolutionary overnight effects. Remember how the advent of talking pictures stood the motion-picture industry on its head? Here is a danger zone which must be watched sharply in these modern times. Techniques and arts change with a speed and violence rarely witnessed in the more leisurely days of the past.

DYNAMITE IN DEPRECIATION AND OBSOLESCENCE

Any machinery or equipment which is subject to rapid wear and tear, or to frequent style changes, should not be bought on the instalment plan. Here also is a lesson for the individual buyer. Goods which are constantly being manipulated by the fashion designers are worrisome instalment obligations. This hits most items of wearing apparel. You may protest that fur coats should be made an exception. Well, perhaps we can pass the fur garments and some other of the more costly articles of apparel. Even on these items, however, it will do no harm to tighten up on terms and scrutinize risks more searchingly. This still leaves untouched the fact that in the apparel field the spurious "ease" with which the easy-payment traps are baited leads to consumer overbuying, and overloading with debt. Proponents of part payments would laugh off such dangers by pointing to the records: the claim is that instalment obligations have come through periods of hard times without showing exceptional distress. Therefore, in response to that apology, I shall now take up further the point that here is a genuine potential danger.

To appreciate what over-expansion of instalment contracts might do to undermine our economy, look back at previous booms. The treacherous character of a boom is due partly to the fact that each boom is likely to be concentrated in a different field than the preceding boom. For illustration, we have seen the country go crazy in railroad booms, land booms, and stock-market booms. The unpredictable element is What will be next? Where will tomorrow's craze strike? One reliable forecast can be made: We know for a practical certainty that the next boom will hit *somewhere*. I expect that a day will come when the temperamental American public will pick a new field for speculative frenzy, and probably this will be the field of partial-payment plans. Some day America is due for an instalment boom. When I say "boom," I mean such a pitch of madness as has swept the historic stock markets and the various real-estate markets. That such a stampede is well within the probabilities is only too evident to anybody who will read the history of booms and crashes.

Many classes of goods obviously are painfully unadapted to instalment buying. An illustration is fresh foods which are subject to immediate deterioration. Some analysts object to livestock as an instalment risk, pointing out the uncertain life expectancy, and the hazards of disease and accident. It would appear that articles used in housekeeping, such as ordinary kitchen utensils, and numerous other low-priced items needed in the modern home, do not properly belong in the instalment category.

It is clear that the social value of a product or service has no necessary relation to its adaptability to the instalment system. Instances in point include: medical services, travel, education and other intangibles. It is no easy matter to organize a complete catalog of household purchases of goods and services, with each item arranged in the order of its suitability for instalment buying. You will at once appreciate that one of the difficulties of such a product is caused by the various uses to which different families may put the same product. For example an automobile may be used in connection with vegetable raising or hell-raising.

Therefore what I propose to do, as the only practical procedure, is to set out the following Analytical Table of the suitability of some typical kinds of goods for instalment practices. This probe is classified under four main divisions: (A) Services or Satisfactions Which Proposed Merchandise Is Expected to Yield; (B) Physical and Financial Characteristics of Proposed Merchandise; (C) Personal Circumstances of the Purchaser; and (D) Outlook for Coming Conditions in Line with Business Cycle. All of those four groups of factors may vitally affect the question whether a proposed purchase is or is not suitable to instalment methods. Next, under each of these four main divisions, I have arranged various sub-divisions. The resulting Analytical Table is not intended to cover all or even a significant proportion of the groups of goods entering into the average family budget. The Table is designed to be used rather as a guide, whereby family deliberations and conferences over a proposed purchase can be organized, systematized and—I hope —reduced to sounder conclusions.

(A) SERVICES OR SATISFACTIONS WHICH THE PROPOSED
MERCHANDISE IS EXPECTED TO YIELD

(1) **Direct Additions to Family Income.** For a farm family the acquisition of a small tractor may demonstrably add to income. Another family living in the suburbs may be convinced that the purchase of modern kitchen equipment would enable the family to take a boarder. The caution here is: Be careful not to fool yourself. It is marvelous, when we are eager to possess something, how we can argue ourselves into feeling that extravagances are economies; that ex-

pense is income; and that a liability is an asset. This is called rationalizing our desires. Watch it.

(2) **Direct Aid in Reducing Expenses.** Sometimes when a desired article cannot be justified on the ground that it will increase income, a case can be built up on the basis that it may save some expenses. It can be argued, for illustration, that perhaps the ownership of equipment for chicken raising would cut down the family's expenses for poultry products. I might feel the tug of any talk about the "economies" from owning a good horse. Hence if I could not buy a horse in any way but by instalments, I might weaken and become quite enthusiastic about the expenses which he would save. We all have such warm spots in our hearts for some particular purchase. That is why our capacities for self-delusion are almost infinite; and why the instalment man will get us if we don't watch out.

(3) **Contributions to Health and Efficiency.** Under this heading come such expenditures as those for surgical, medical, and dental services. When analyzing this kind of expenditure, probably we are less likely to indulge in hocus-pocus and "kidding ourselves." Moreover this is not a field which has yet been invaded appreciably by the unscrupulous among the instalment operators.

(4) **Educational Value.** In the same way that some desired expenditure can be discussed with respect to its probable contribution to health, we can investigate possibilities of increasing our store of wisdom. I am not disposed to pick a quarrel with the instalment pur-

chase of education. Here, however, it is not amiss to extend warning on the question of persistency. Education is one of those pursuits in which there are many who start and far fewer who finish. Unless a family is convinced that the favored one will see it through, is it judicious to undertake a contract for education, however admirable and laudable it may be in purpose?

(5) **Help in Character Building.** Finally we arrive at this fifth consideration which may influence our decision on a prospective purchase on instalments. Undoubtedly many things can be suggested on the pleas that their possession will contribute to the up-building of character. The supreme importance of spiritual values is something which I have been preaching for the larger part of a lifetime. As an individual, family and national asset, nothing can be found to compare with character. Nevertheless, I raise this question. Does instalment buying, as practiced by the average family, tend on the whole to improve or impair character? To me it seems inconsistent to propose buying something to build character and in the same breath to countenance a *method* of buying which may undermine character.

(B) PHYSICAL AND FINANCIAL CHARACTERISTICS OF
PROPOSED MERCHANDISE

(1) **Price.** One reason why automobile financing has made such rapid progress is that the automobile is a relatively costly article. A finance company incurs certain routine expenses in taking on an account; and a considerable share of such expenses must be borne

whether the article is of small or big value. It costs the finance company about as much to handle a cheap as a high-priced article. Obviously it is more efficient that the amount of unit sale should be fairly large. It is expensive to look up a customer's credit standing, set up the accounting material for handling his account, and take care of the collections. For such routine to be justified, means that each account should run into reasonably heavy volume. You cannot expect the finance companies to carry you in the purchase of a stick of gum on instalments. Therefore, the instalment field should at least be limited to the major rather than the minor items of the family budget.

(2) **Life Expectancy — Depreciation.** Consider, for example, the oil-burning equipment for a home. The life expectancy of such equipment, if of good grade, is a matter of many years. If the instalment contract is made for a reasonable duration, it may be cleaned up far in advance of the final write-off of the goods. This suggests as a sort of formula for instalment sales: *the mortality of the product* should outlast the *maturity of the contract* by a liberal *margin of safety*.

(3) **Life Expectancy—Obsolescence.** Merchandise which is contemplated as a purchase on instalments should also be scrutinized from this angle of obsolescence. This means, of course, that some merchandise quickly becomes of small commercial value, not because of wear and tear, but because of changing styles and fashions. To the enemies which the Scriptures enumerate as "moth and rust," we of the modern

generations must add as further foes the whims, manipulations of dictatorial designers, money-mad manufacturers, and conscienceless store-keepers. The modern generations have been "conditioned" by pitiless publicity-men to accept as true values the sheer nonsense of the style rackets. Therefore most lines of apparel, especially in women's wear, should not be bought on instalments. They are built to dash out of date as soon as possible. If the instalment industry protests at our classification of apparel as a product which should not be bought by part payments, do not condemn *us*. The culprit is not the analyst but rather those who pervert style into a knife to cut the throats of innocent women and children.

(4) **Terms of Contract.** Obviously the decision whether or not to make a contemplated purchase on instalments, will be governed in part by the proffered terms of the contract. The bones of such a contract include among the various other provisions: (a) Down payment; (b) Rate of interest (be sure that you figure correctly the actual effective rate and do not take for granted the correctness of the nominal quoted rate); (c) Repossession value (for example, a set of artificial teeth may have high value in situ but the repossession value is low); and (d) Maturity or duration of the contract. Remember that in the long run the terms of contracts for various classes of goods will become adjusted by trial-and-error to reflect the average credit experiences of the finance companies. Just as insurance rates tend to embody the underwriters' experience and expectancy statistics, so instalment terms are

molded by instalment history. This means that on
certain kinds of articles you are probably being forced
to pay for the short-comings of generations of bad
debtors, as the careful automobile drivers have to pay
higher rates of insurance because of damages done by
reckless drivers. The moral is that whenever the terms
inflicted on a given product seem unduly harsh, be on
your guard. Such severity may be a signal that if you
sign such a contract you may be penalized for the past
misconduct of other debtors.

Mr. Boake Carter gives us The Tale of the Mink
Coat. Two young ladies, he reports, were attracted
to a mink coat in a furrier's window. Entering the
store, they were shown the garment and the salesman
was eloquent on its loveliness. Finally he led up skill-
fully to the question of price. Whereupon the young
ladies exclaimed, almost in unison:

"Oh, we are not interested in the price. All that we
want to know is the amount of the down payment!"

(c) PERSONAL CIRCUMSTANCES OF THE PURCHASER

Consideration of this section of our Analytical Table
shows why it is difficult to make up a dogmatic dic-
tionary of articles which should *not* be bought on
instalments. What is meat to one family may be
poison to another. A curious commentary on human
nature is that the wealthy and well-to-do, who are
logically the qualified candidates for instalment buying
are *psychologically* the quickest to detect its dangers.
Are their aversion to "getting stuck" and their love of
lower prices for cash two of the secrets of how the

wealthy have accumulated their wealth, and how the well-to-do have done well?

Probably the chief mistake made by families tempted into instalment excesses is to assume that their present comfortable or easy circumstances will last forever. Once when a family with slender income had contrived to put up a pretentious country house, Fred Allen suggested that an imposing name for the lordly estate would be: "Teetering-On-The-Brink." Contracts which might be handled readily in a present situation may become burdensome or intolerable in the near future through some sudden shift in the family's economic conditions. Although the average family must realize perfectly that today is different from yesterday, it still persists in feeling that tomorrow will be like today—or better. Let us cherish the right kind of optimism, knowing that futile worrying tends to impair health and to give us a real cause for worry. The only final security is courage. This is good, sound, and wholesome philosophy.

Frank facing of the family's true situation in all its details—pecuniary income and resources, health, and spiritual stamina—this is the only safe and sound way to approach the problem of whether to buy or not to buy. Family ages are a factor of great significance. The youthful have surplus energies, although they may also have surplus expenses. Whereas the middle-aged may be over the peak of the unavoidable loads upon their incomes, this age group is usually less aggressive in hustling for additional sources to meet emergencies. Men usually feel that they are better equipped to "gamble" than are women. Though partly a matter of temperament, this has some basis of truth.

I am told that last winter a neighborly group of Massachusetts people were playing cards one evening. Suddenly they were startled to hear on the door the thunderings of the police. The hostess rushed to open the door and a tough cop stuck in his head and bawled:

"Who is the owner of this car out here parked in front of the hydrant?"

A worried little man hopped up from the card table.

"Please, officer," he piped, "the pup on the back seat is mine but the car is the Mercantile Credit Company's, and the overcoat tied around the radiator belongs to the Citizen's Budget Corporation."

I am ashamed that was a Massachusetts family as I was born and brought up in that State. The State symbol of Massachusetts is the codfish. We love that fish, for we believe that COD stood for Cash On Delivery. It will be a bad day for the old Commonwealth if too large numbers of the population learn to laugh at the COD and salute the SUCKER.

Probably a safe rule is this: any family which is already carrying one instalment contract should never assume another until the first one has been paid up in full.

The attendants in charge of zoölogical gardens have learned about the habit of the boa constrictor. They tell me that in handling a healthy, adult boa, the following formula is worth remembering. When a boa starts swinging coils around a man: one coil, danger; two coils, deadly peril; three coils, sure death. If you cannot keep your family entirely clear of the instalment constrictor, at least limit it to one coil.

(D) OUTLOOK FOR COMING CONDITIONS IN LINE WITH BUSINESS CYCLE

A proposed purchase on instalments may offer real opportunities for increasing income or cutting expenses. Undeniably it may promise to enhance health, extend education and improve character. The terms of the proposed contract may seem honest and favorable. The family may appear to be amply well-situated to take care of such a transaction. Every other section of our Analytical Table may give an encouraging indication when probing the contemplated instalment contract. However, what about this final and critical inquiry into the trend of fundamental conditions and the business cycle? You have only to consult the pages of history to be overwhelmingly convinced that here are all-powerful forces. Families which for generations have occupied a position that seemed impregnable have been crashed into the gutter by the impact of panics and depressions. The danger that such a cyclical catastrophe from the outside may strike down your family is much less at a time when business is at low ebb and far under its line of normal growth. Hence if you ever buy on the instalment plan select a time of depression.

The dangers of an economic thunderstorm are especially pronounced during times of speculative booms. The only safe policy which a family can follow during prosperous periods is to avoid making instalment contracts on *any* kind of merchandise. Wisdom at such times consists of getting out of debt altogether. Such getting out of debt is like equipping your house with adequate lightning rods. With that Get-Out-of-Debt protection you can face a thunderstorm with comparative assurance of your own safety. Debts seem to attract the economic bolts as certain physical objects are known to attract lightning. During a severe electrical storm no person of intelligence would choose to go out into a bare field and chain himself to an iron plow. Such dare-devil flouting of well-known scientific laws is no more defiant than the parallel behavior of families in boomtimes. Both kinds of fools are courting destruction.

FEWER THINGS SHOULD BE BOUGHT

Some years ago if you had listed the products suitable for instalment buying you might have made up a rather long list. Today such a catalog is far shorter. Tomorrow the list may even be briefer. The reasons why the list of things suitable for instalment selling is ever shortening is that many industries have adopted the systematic policy of deliberately making their products "softer." Plenty of items of modern merchandising could be designed and built to give years of additional service. That, however, looks like bad business. To stimulate sales, so some manufacturers reason, the trick is to construct the goods so they will wear out and have to be replaced as fast as possible. Therefore we have at play two conflicting forces. Acting in one direction is the drive for instalment sales, which by rights require that the goods should be high-valued and long-lived. Acting in the opposite direction is the modern tendency to "soften" goods, a policy which makes them less appropriate for instalment purchasing.

Another influence of similar type is likewise tending to deteriorate the character of merchandise as suitable material for instalment contracts. This is the tendency of manufacturers and designers to intensify the style factor. Fashion and style are being introduced into fields which formerly were ruled by pure utility. Even such products as machine tools, for example, are being streamlined, not in the main for functional purposes but to add eye-appeal. Where style changes have been slow, the tendency is to speed up these senseless switches. While pushing the rapid-wear idea in their products, some makers go still further: what is not out-worn soon enough must be out-moded. Of course every such move in this direction tends to create merchandise that is unsuitable for any sound purchasing on instalments. Such contracts, to be permissible, should be applied only to goods in which durability is at a maximum and the style factor at a minimum.

DANGEROUS MIS-EDUCATION THROUGH VICIOUS ADS

One of the severest indictments of advertising is based on its tendency to corrupt the public's desires. Normally the public has much common sense and sound instincts. At enormous costs some of the advertisers have succeeded in breaking down the people's natural good judgment and debauching their demands.

For illustration, in certain sections of the cosmetic industries, it would appear that much of the price which the consumer pays is for meretricious and fanciful values. She pays—under the spell of hypnotic advertising—for excessively ornate packaging, for an extortionate expense of distribution, for gyps in quantities and qualities—and for the very publicity which exploits her. Under the super-pressure of advertising there has been developed a mass of false standards, spurious values, and artificial appeals. Much of this flood of modern merchandise has well been called counterfeit. A shocking percentage of the dollar the consumer pays, represents alleged values which actually are fakes if judged by rational standards.

A further trend is steadily lessening the list of goods which properly can be bought on partial-payment plans. I have in mind the fast and accelerating progress of invention and discovery. False and injurious obsolescence is created by degrading the quality of goods; it is also created by over-emphasizing the style factor. However, there is another obsolescence. This results from genuine work of the research men and technicians in improving goods along scientific lines. When the color of apparel is changed from blue to red, or vice-versa, merely as an artificial style-stimulant to sales, this is scarcely better than outright trickery. On the contrary, when the handles of valves, for illustration, are colored blue and red to facilitate recognition and operation, that is a sincere step forward. That is service to humanity, whereas much of "styling" is disservice. Nevertheless, no matter how beneficent, invention and discovery are making obsolescence more rapid. They are increasing the number of goods which should *not* be purchased on instalments.

Many basic trends, then, are affecting the field of merchandising and steadily curtailing the area which can properly be claimed as suitable for instalment buying. Among such trends, four have been outlined: (1) The policy of some manufacturers, aided and abetted by their leaders, purposely to degrade the quality of their goods so that consumers will be compelled to buy more often; (2) Injection of arbitrary, useless, and expensive style and color factors, so that goods will quickly go out of date and consumers will be tempted to make premature replacements; (3) Cultivation, through high-pressure publicity, of foolish standards, false appetites, careless buying and acceptance of poor quality merchandise; (4) The speed-up of obsolescence through the honest and solid accomplishments of the technicians. Each and all of those four basic trends tend to lessen the number of kinds of goods which consumers should—under any conditions—buy on the instalment plan. Let me further add, it would be well for the leaders of this instalment business not to resent constructive analysis and criticism such as I have endeavored to present. If inclined at first to resent such suggestions, let these leaders observe that their logical zone of operations is persistently shrinking through the action of fundamental forces. Time is working against the instalment operators.

SUMMARY AND CONCLUSIONS

Pointing up the foregoing analysis, we can now attempt a listing of some typical classes of merchandise. Thus we answer the question heading this chapter: When and What NOT to Buy on Instalments. Beware of such pitfalls as the following:

1. Goods of low unit price.
   (Illustrations: Cheap clothes, tawdry jewelry, flimsy radios.)
2. Goods with low or practically no repossession value.
   (Illustrations: Foods, supplies, travel trips.)
3. Goods with a high rate of depreciation and obsolescence.
   (Illustrations: Frail furniture, shoddy tires, apparel in extreme fashions.)
4. Goods specially custom-built-to-order to meet individual ideas rather than of standard mass-consumption designs.
   (Illustrations: Tailored clothing, freak houses, sport automobiles with equipment carried to extremes.)
5. Goods that lower income, increase expense, or fail to render some real economic service.
   (Illustrations: Automobiles priced beyond family's financial and social position, lavish and extravagant entertainment, touring and travel

without worthwhile objectives and marked by dissipation.)

6. Goods that make no contribution to health, intelligence and character, or actually impair these assets.

7. Goods that are offered on a ridiculously inadequate down payment.

8. Goods that tempt with an unduly prolonged maturity of contract.

9. Goods that impose usurious charges when the true rate of interest is figured.

10. Goods that are inconsistent with family's situation and outlook.

11. Goods that the family has no business to buy in view of the burden of prior contracts which have been already assumed by the family.

12. Goods that are bought in the heights of a business boom.

In all probability this book will be misunderstood, misinterpreted, and misrepresented. For stating frankly and flatly what I really believe, I shall probably be smeared with protests and criticisms. For me that will be no novel experience. Moreover, it will be a trivial price to pay if the book leads the members of even one family to stop and think before they slap their signatures on a bad contract and sell themselves down the river of debt.

"He that buys upon credit, pays interest for what he buys, and he that pays ready money, might let that money out to use; so that he that possesses anything he has bought, pays interest for the use of it. In buying goods, it is best to pay ready money, because he that sells upon credit expects to lose five per cent by bad debts; therefore he charges on all he sells upon credit, an advance that shall make up that deficiency. Those who pay for what they buy upon credit, pay their share of this advance. He that pays ready money, escapes, or may escape, that charge."

> "A penny saved is two pence clear,
> A pin a day's a groat a year."

The above advice was published some 150 years ago, over the modest signature "B. Franklin."

CHAPTER NINE

INSTALMENT SELLING IN GREAT BRITAIN

"Debt is like any other trap; easy to get into but
hard to get out of."—*Shaw*

"Debt is the prolific mother of folly and crime."
—*Disraeli*

The author of the Book of Ecclesiastes wrote 2500
years ago: "There is no new thing under the sun."
This apparently applies to buying things on the instalment plan. I arrive at that conclusion for the following reason. Recently when visiting the British House
of Parliament in London, I saw some sticks in a glass
case. Upon inquiring what they were, I was told that
they are part of an ancient book-keeping system used
several hundred years ago. Upon further inquiry at
the British Museum, I learned this remarkable fact.
I found that things were bought and sold on ten
monthly payments as early as Cromwell's time—yes,
and even before the days of paper, ink, and formal
arithmetic!

Readers will be interested in knowing how these records of instalment payments were kept. The little
sticks of wood exhibited in one of the corridors of the
House of Parliament explain the method. These pieces
of wood are about an inch wide, eight inches long, and

a quarter of an inch thick. For every one of the ten payments which the instalment purchaser made, a groove about one sixteenth of an inch deep was cut across the flat face of the stick. This stick was originally given to him when he made his first payment and was brought back by him to the seller whenever making an additional payment. When ten of these grooves had been cut, it showed that the ox, plow, or whatever else had been purchased on the instalment plan was paid for in full.

You may ask, however, "What prevented the buyer from cutting grooves himself, when he had not made payments?" Well, the people of those times were not fools even before the days of reading, writing and arithmetic. Here is the explanation. The stick originally was two inches wide instead of one inch wide; and the first groove was cut across the full two-inch face of the stick. Then the stick was split lengthwise into two approximately equal parts. One part was retained by the seller and one part was given to the buyer. When an additional payment was made, the two parts of the original stick were fitted together; and the new groove was made across the original two-inch face. This meant that any groove on the buyer's half which did not appear also on the seller's half, did not count. Furthermore, when sticks were split, the splitting was never twice alike, and hence it was impossible to forge a dishonest duplicate.

The foregoing illustration is but one of the multitude of interesting and significant mementos of the development of business. Great Britain especially is a veritable treasure house of exhibits fascinating to the student of economic evolution. In fact, each year I now try to visit England, where it is possible to meet many people from all over the world. One can learn almost as much about world affairs by spending a month in London as by traveling many months in Europe. This is particularly true in the case of one who has not a ready use of foreign languages.

But I confess to the further reason why I like to visit England: to get new ideas on trading methods. The English may not be very good manufacturers, but they are great merchants and bankers. They trade violently both with themselves and with all nations. In every port in the world will be found English ships; while the number of stores, per thousand population, is probably greater in England than in any other country. It is not surprising, therefore, that the instalment business secured a strong foothold there. In England, however, buying on instalments is known as buying on the "hire-purchase" plan. Therefore, this is the term which I shall use in this chapter.

"HIRE-PURCHASE" PLANS

Once when in England, I asked how this name hire-purchase plan ever started. I was told: "You see, one group of merchants wanted to call it the 'hire plan,' while another group wanted to call it the 'purchase plan.' As we English are great for compromising, we agree on the name 'hire-purchase.' This suits everyone."

If in England you get into a motor bus, you will see

staring you in the face an advertisement to buy things —from cradles to coffins—on the hire-purchase plan. Once when I asked a bus conductor what he thought of this plan of buying, he replied, "If it's heads, the seller wins; while if it's tails, the buyer loses." Then he asked, "Did you ever hear of the merchant and customer who bought the cow together—on equal partnership? Each had half of the cow; but it was soon found that the storekeeper had taken the hind half which gave the milk; while the customer had the front half which had to be fed! Well—when you don't pay cash, you are buying the front end of a cow! The hire-purchase plan, moreover, is a mighty hungry cow."

The development of the instalment business was of slow but insidious growth in Great Britain. Before the World War that growth was retarded by the meager *per unit* purchasing power of the masses. The natural conservatism of the average Briton was the traditional principle of paying one's way and eschewing debt. The successive post-war recoveries from depression however were accompanied by rapid expansions of business done in an increasing variety of articles on the basis of hire-purchase. The recovery from the great world slump of 1929-1935 was followed by even more rapid developments in hire-purchase. These were both astounding and disturbing to those watching the course of economic life in England, Scotland and Wales. It penetrated many new lines of business while at the same time it gained greatly in volume in those lines where it had earlier secured entrenchment.

HIGH-PRESSURE SELLING

The principle of "possess today and pay tomorrow, or when and if you can," is found impinging on the British mind (and morals) from many angles of economic and social life. A detailed criticism of hire-purchase, in its innumerable phases and effects, would fill a huge volume. Consider but one of these many angles, advertising. Every billboard, every newspaper, periodical or magazine, the cinema, the theater —all play a part. No mind can escape the ceaselessly operating suggestive force of instalment buying. A million messages are crowded on the sight by day and night through these media in the development of which the best brains of every form of publicity are engaged. On this, the selling side of the campaign, we must remember the salesman, not forgetting the "high-pressure" gentleman of that calling. Specialization in all branches of business is the tendency in these times, and the salesman is necessarily a specialized product.

No one would adversely criticize the reputable specialized salesman with his training in the psychology of potential buyers and the like. A criticism of hire-purchase is necessarily directed towards the principle itself. One may discover a measure of sympathy with those who, being in business, are compelled to adjust themselves to business trends and tendencies over which they can have no control. Publicity, the salesman, and the finance house which specializes in discounting hire-purchase "paper" have, however, played their part. They steadily undermined the old-fashioned resistance of the average Briton to entering into money contracts which may dangerously discount his future purchasing power.

DEADLY DRAINS ON PURCHASING POWER

In considering the effects of a large-scale growth of the hire-purchase contract in regard to any given nation, the outstanding effect and medium for misgiving is that of the inroad made into the purchasing power of the masses. The British wage-earner, whose modest few pounds a week is spent on his family, is the real basis of the rapid exchange of goods and services. Therefore he is the fundamental factor of what we call prosperity. The essential of maintaining the nation's income at a high level is that income should mainly be expended on the products of the field and industry. To save a proportion of income is protective and sound; but it is expenditure on goods and services giving the greatest measure of employment which keeps the wheels of economy turning. It is the family man, or woman, of modest income who is the vital factor in mass spending. Therefore, how vital it must be that he, or she, should get the keenest value for money spent. It further follows that every intervening trading interest which seeks to over-exploit its position must do so to the detriment of the person of modest income and hence to the detriment of the nation as a whole.

Does hire-purchase over-exploit its position? Does it, as a truly modern departure in business, imply drain on the people's purchasing power? Does it mean that a person obligated under hire-purchase contracts will at the end of a year find himself worse off in terms of goods and services than he would have been under a system of fairly-priced, cash purchases? The answer to these questions is undoubtedly in the affirmative.

Fifty years ago the production of all goods and services in England was in actual short supply, meaning that millions of people had to go without. Today science and mass production have reached a critical stage. The struggle between the pressure of unbounded potential production and the people's ability to pay for it clash. The basic fact of economic life has changed from shortage to plenitude. Industrially, mass production took its greatest stride following the first post-war slump. Money, as a purchasing power, stood in the way of absorbing the vast volumes of goods which machinery and efficiency were waiting to turn out. Here stepped in the complementary principle of hire-purchase. In theory, hire-purchase gave the British people the purchasing power, or credit, which they lacked in order to complete the circuit of boundless production and ceaseless absorption. In practice, it developed into a medium designedly depriving the people of varying proportions of income. The hire-purchase contract embodies the cankerous principle of compound interest; vastly increases advertising costs, for which the consumer pays; and additionally imposes on him the costly intervening medium of the discount house.

THE LAW INTERVENES—SCANDALOUS ABUSES!

In the Parliamentary debate late in 1937 on the Second Reading of the Hire-Purchase Bill, speakers were careful to discriminate between reputable firms carrying on business under hire-purchase contracts and firms which, to judge by references to them and their methods during the debate, were anything but reputable. I, however, allow for discrimination and accept the distinction drawn between reputable and disreputable. It has to be remembered also, in criticizing the principle of hire-purchase as a whole, that the business has grown to the proportions of a huge vested interest. Consequently, it is hardly to be expected that the projected Bill was intended to do, or could do, other than seek the elimination of certain abuses. These, protected as they were by law, became a scandal in the mind of the public.

The Bill did not touch upon the debatable question concerning the widespread adoption of hire-purchase as a principle in our economic life, and the weighing of the benefits of the system against the obvious dangers it carries. The debate suggested tacit recognition of the fact that hire-purchase, as a deeply entrenched institution of our times, had come to stay. This disappointed those who expected a thorough ventilation of the real incidence of hire-purchase on the lives of the masses by the depletion of purchasing power through a general mortgaging of their uncertain future. The importance of the question as a whole will be seen from this statement made in the House of Commons: "On competent authority, no less than 5,000,000 British families are in the clutches of this system for furniture and clothing alone." If we remember how many other products—houses, motor-cars, machinery, etc.—depend largely on hire-purchase, the seriousness becomes apparent. It will then be realized how deeply hire-purchase, both the reputable and disreputable types, has invaded British business and domestic life.

SWINDLERS PROTECTED AND ENCOURAGED

It may be of interest to consider the particular instances of abuse to which attention was drawn in the debate on the Bill itself. What is known as the "snatchback" firm is a firm which is anxious to repossess goods sold under hire-purchase contracts in order that they may be sold again, frequently as new goods. Actually, goods changing hands under hire-purchase remain the property of the retailing interest until the contract is completed in all respects. Then the person "hiring" has the option to "purchase outright" at a nominal figure, say one shilling. Such a contract provides golden opportunities for the firm anxious to withdraw goods when a major proportion of instalments has been paid thereon. It can then again "hire out" the same goods to fresh "purchasers." I was informed that in a certain provincial city of England more than 500 wireless sets had been withdrawn from hirers, the average instalment payments made per unit being more than 25 per cent. One trader stated that he had sold a set for the eighth time at the original price! A bedroom suite was stated to have been bought by a retailer for £5. 15. o. and disposed of under hire-purchase for £19.

Another instance of the sharp practice possible under hire-purchase: A poor woman bought furniture to the amount of £27. 1. 9., default on payments arising when £25. 16. 9. had been paid off. Prosecution followed, resulting in costs against her of £6. 8. 9. While the woman was out charing, the goods were removed with £5 worth of other goods for court costs! A further instance was of forcible removal, a "bruiser" being on hand and dealing effectively with opposition while the goods wanted were removed. Fortunately, the assailants were fined for assault, but it is pointed out that in innumerable cases unfortunate hirers are either too poor or too terrorized to take action. The disreputable retailer continually oversteps the legal limits of his power.

MORE TRICKS OF THE TRADE

Then there is the "linked-on" hire-purchase system. A contract for, say £25 of furniture may be on the verge of completion. The salesman calls round and induces the hirer to contract for additional goods. The second lot of goods is then linked on to the first lot, thus making a single contract. Instalments on the second lot may be about a third paid when the hirer gets out of work and can not keep up the instalments. Despite the fact that the first lot of goods are entirely paid for, both the first and second deliveries are legally repossessed and the hirer loses both his money and the goods.

The case of the foolish woman who cannot say "No" to the blandishments of the high-pressure, house-to-house canvasser for orders under hire-purchase agreements, is unfortunately all too common. These unhappy women sign agreements which they hardly read and certainly do not understand them if they do read them. I was told of a woman obtaining the goods, hiding the knowledge of them from her husband, pawning them to pay the instalments and, in despair, committing suicide. A letter from an experienced supplier read: "I have trained hundreds of men to overcome wives' objections and sales resistance against signing documents when their husbands are not present." Here is an outstanding instance of salesman enterprise. A poor woman was induced to sign a contract for a vacuum cleaner when she had nothing to clean and where the salesman completed the deal by paying the first instalment himself. The unfortunate hirer was subsequently continuously badgered for instalments, even her relatives being brought into the matter.

A particularly enterprising hire-purchase firm is on record as leaving the space for the amount of the purchase in the agreement blank till after the signatures were obtained when an amount in excess of the verbally stated sum was subsequently filled in. Depreciation appears to be something which greatly favors the seller under the law as it stood in 1937. Fortunately, it is a matter which the Hire-Purchase Bill sought to revise. If, for example, a wireless set is proved inefficient after delivery it could be returned only on the terms of depreciation stated in the contract. *The*

Court of Appeal handed down a decision that 80 per cent of the total value of the goods is a fair and reasonable proportion to cover depreciation! A wireless set on being returned, following argument on its efficiency, cannot depreciate much in a week; yet in many instances, the hirer has had to pay two-thirds of the original price and give up the set.

DEFENDANTS THAT CANNOT DEFEND. THE LINK WITH THE MONEY-LENDER

It is difficult to understand how hire-purchase law can have been left so long unassailed by healthy and effectual criticism. The unfairness manifest is not only notoriously obvious, but it has paved the way for protected abuses. These cannot possibly have been foreseen originally as they should have been by an experienced intelligence. Consider the fact that goods may be sold to people living hundreds of miles from where the suppliers are located. Proceedings against hirers can be taken at courts in distant cities where the retailers carry on business. This often makes it impossible for unfortunate debtors to defend themselves. Judgment in such cases goes by default, the plaintiffs, of course, having matters all their own way. Money-lending is said to be linked up with the more questionable forms of hire-purchase business in England. A hirer asks for grace when in temporary difficulties and subsequently receives a communication from a professional money-lender. The Irish Free State Commission, investigating hire-purchase in that country, came to the conclusion that hire-purchase is better described as a money-lending system than as a trading system.

THE INCOMPREHENSIBLE CONTRACT—LOOPHOLES IN THE LAW

The manner in which hire-purchase agreements are set out would certainly suggest to the normal mind a skillful plan to make comprehension difficult. The less vital clauses are printed boldly. Those containing, as it were, the crux of the matter are frequently in exceedingly small type and involved in context. A learned judge expressed the opinion that hire-purchase contracts were complex but well drawn. Rarely could a loophole be found for the purpose of affording relief to a harassed hirer.

A bill to regulate instalment purchases properly should be wide enough in scope to deal with the wiliness of the disreputable firm in continuing its practices through loopholes left in the law. The 1932 Hire-Purchase Bill for Scotland, a measure intended to revise the law in order to give more protection to the hirer, was greatly abused. Certain hire-purchase companies affected merely transferred their business system from hire-purchase agreements to credit-sales agreements. Thereupon the hoped-for benefits to hirers from the Scottish Bill were lost. It is to be inferred that unless a Bill is made exceedingly water-tight, ways and means will be found by certain interests to neutralize intended benefits for the public.

It may come as a surprise to many to know that, after 1935, agriculture very largely "went on hire-purchase." One aspect of the position, particularly affecting agriculture, is that of farmers who acquired cattle which, unknown to them, had been the subject of hire-purchase. They had paid for cattle in good faith, when along came the hire-purchase company and demanded delivery of the stock. The farmers lost both the stock and their money. Clearly, hire-purchase companies have been in a privileged position. Auctioneers are stated to lose considerable sums of money every year by innocently selling goods which are still the property of hire-purchase companies. In such instances, actions for damages were in favor of the hire-purchase companies, despite the unquestioned good faith of the auctioneer. It is suggested that it was the hire-purchase companies which originally put the goods in the position of appearing to belong to a party to whom they do not belong!

MISREPRESENTATION AND HIGH-PRESSURE SALESMANSHIP

Legislation should cover possible misrepresentation by salesmen. It has to be remembered that the salesman, agent, or tout, as the case may be, has probably been specially trained to sell goods to anyone. This means whether people have a real need of them or not. He is taught to sell regardless of adequate capacity to pay. The vital point from the salesman's point of view is to effect a sale: it is his living to sell. On the other hand, the potential customer has had no training in the art, so difficult to many, of refusing to be badgered into acquiring something which he does not

want. It is not enough to say that the "victim" of
the salesman's attack has the right of the free-born
Briton to refuse a contract.

Hard facts show that innumerable people can be
engineered into ceding their signatures, bitterly to regret later having done so. The trained mental force
of the high-pressure salesman, fighting fiercely for his
living, is undoubtedly responsible for many thousands
of deeply regretted hire-purchase contracts. That force
can, and often does, amount to a measure of hypno-
tism. There exist known instances of experienced business men allowing themselves to be "talked" into foolish agreements. Later, they have been at a loss to
understand how they could have committed themselves.
If high-pressure salesmanship can have such triumphs,
it is not difficult to imagine the innumerable successes
obtained when the concentrated force is directed on
inexperienced and uneducated people. The path to
possession is painted in such rosy terms, with the
thorns of possession so cleverly hidden, that it is very
difficult not to be caught. Truly, it may be said that
business enterprise taking on so low and reprehensible
a garb is unworthy of the name of business. It would
better be described as criminal intent.

It is, of course, unfair even in the case of the worst
type of salesman, to throw on him all the blame for
unworthily inducing signatures to unexplained hire-
purchase contracts. A number of companies, however,
are undoubtedly directly responsible for the questionable methods employed by their representatives. The
worst type of companies pay only a very nominal wage

to the salesman. This wage is paid merely to permit charging the salesman with embezzlement should collection troubles arise. This charge the company could not make were the basis of remuneration by commission only. The living of the salesman thus depends on his commissions via a number of contracts which will be honored for at least two or three instalments. The temptation for a salesman working under such conditions is obvious. He must make "sales" at all costs if he is to eat. Human nature being what it is, misrepresentation of one type or another is thus resorted to all too frequently.

REVISION OF THE LAW LEAVES THE MAJOR PROBLEM UNTOUCHED

The foregoing indicates that legislation must deal in some measure with the many and more obvious abuses of the hire-purchase system. I surely hope that laws in process of enactment will suffice to minimize the gross evils which have been exposed. The vital issue of the system itself, however, is apt to be left untouched. Powerful firms will still continue to charge for their goods prices which show enormous increases on prime costs. It is said, for example, that the manufacturing cost of a certain English vacuum cleaner is £2 per machine; while the cost to the public, under hire-purchase, is in the region of £18. This of course includes the salesman's commission. A certain English manufacturer and retailer of wireless equipment produced sets well under £2 each. These were placed at the service of customers for ultimate purchase at around £20 per set. In such cases the public pays for enormously expanded advertising necessitated by competition. It is significant to note, moreover, that such competition does not bring down the price. The various firms are linked by the common motive of making the people pay.

Then there is the discount house, or hire-purchase finance company, which may want up to twenty-five per cent for its services. There is also the luxury of uncomprehended compound interest to be paid by the customer. The disclosed profits of these companies which manufacture and sell to the public are no indication of real profits. Legitimate methods of financial conduct over a period of years can make current dividends appear satisfactorily modest. By the strict conservation of funds retained for expenditure within the business, and by the capitalization of such reserves, the books can be made to show about what the companies want to show.

HIRE-PURCHASE CONTINUES TO UNDERMINE PROSPERITY

The fact remains that if a company can manufacture goods subject to competition at £2 and sell them for £20 apiece, the drain on the purchasing power of the people must be little less than appalling. Yet there are thousands of companies said to be doing similar business in England. The greater part of the spread between such costs of goods and such sale prices goes into the pockets of vested business interests. Such interests do not, for the most part, spend their takings. A proportion of the "spread" is consolidated, much of

it as investments abroad. Were these funds returned
to the business and the trading world, the purchasing
power might thereby be maintained. This would not
be so serious a matter. Actually, the system at work
is a process of depleting the masses of their true spending power. In the first instance, this takes place by
the enormous spread between prime costs and selling
prices under hire-purchase contracts. In the second
instance, it occurs by immobilizing a persistent percentage of funds obtained from such sales.

It is this process of depleting the people's purchasing
power and the non-return of a percentage of that purchasing power to the people from whom it came that
may be the underlying cause of the next great depression. The enormous growth of hire-purchase lends
wings to the process despite any temporary relief given
to the masses by post-war inflation. It is useless to
raise wages, to keep cash prices down, to provide work
and to lever up the standard of living while this drain
is going on. This drain is being accentuated through
the medium of educating the people to accept an inde-
fensible debtor attitude as if it were honorable and
common to all. The hire-purchase contract, and all for
which it stands, is clearly a method of killing the British goose that lays the golden egg.

CHAPTER TEN

Buy Only for Cash

"The second vice is lying; the first vice is owing. Some men are known by their deeds, others by their mortgages."
— *Anonymous*

Bankers of the old school were taught that a loan to purchase goods for the purpose of *consumption* was a bad loan. Loans were made to facilitate the *production* and *distribution* of raw materials and finished goods. Credit was extended to the business man because he added to the value of the raw materials, semi-finished goods, or completed articles that passed through his hands. If such a loan went bad the business man had assets which were saleable.

A banker who loaned to a consumer was considered beyond the pale by banking standards of 1910. Two reasons were advanced to back up this policy. In the first place a man who borrowed for consumption was adjudged a spendthrift. He was a poor moral risk. A loan to him was a violation of all the principles of sound credit. The other reason advanced was more practical. If the loan should go bad, the assets of the bankrupt were not readily saleable. Once an article goes into the hands of a consumer, it depreciates tremendously. There would be nothing of much value upon which the banker could realize.

Beneath these reasons there was a more fundamental one. The banker then had the credit field to himself. He had no Uncle Sam in the banking business as his competitor. He was a real monopoly in himself. He was the Court of Last Appeal. There was no RFC to step in and take care of a borrower whom the banker had turned down. There was plenty of demand from big borrowers. Their business could be handled without a mass of detail. In a word, there was no need to bother with the *small fry!*

Let us take a look and see how the banker has changed his mind about the ethics of loaning money to a consumer. Not far from my home in Gloucester there is a small-town banker whom I know well. He has a good reputation in his own community. His bank went through the dark days of 1932-33 without calling on the Government for aid. His was always the last word as to whether a loan would be made or a bond purchased. Shortly after general business began to pick up from the severe depression, this banker was approached by a larger institution that wanted to include his bank in a combine that was being formed. The picture painted was an attractive one. Many benefits would accrue to his home town. Greater banking facilities would be brought to the very doors of his fellow citizens.

My friend was growing old. He could still retain his position as apparent head of the bank, but his responsibilities would largely be assumed by the man-

agement of the larger institution. He became sold on
the idea himself and worked hard on his fellow directors to persuade them to sell out the bank to the combine. The price was attractive and the deal was made.
My friend remained as titular head of the bank which
now became a branch of the larger institution. However, he learned before long that some of the loan practices he had considered good money makers, and sound
too, were found to be unorthodox in the eyes of the
new management. After all he was only a country
banker and he did not object to the new rules as they
were enforced.

One day orders came from headquarters to discon-
tinue all loans to certain local merchants. These loans
financed such things as radios, washing machines and
refrigerators. Headquarters believed this was not desirable business; that it was a consumer type of loan
and should be left to the finance companies. Now the
type of loan which was frowned upon by the home
office of the large bank had never shown my friend's
bank a single dollar of loss. Such loans, to be sure,
were of the same type that many a finance company
was making; but they had been made to men whom
my friend considered progressive local merchants.
Moreover, the loans represented two-name paper—
they bore both the signature of the refrigerator purchaser and the endorsement of the local merchant who
sold the refrigerator. Then, there was another angle:
the loans were made at a lower net cost to the borrower than any financial company was offering. It was
good business and a real service.

However, "orders were orders." As the merchants' paper matured it was paid off and the business went to the local branch office of an instalment finance company. My banker was perplexed, but the main office comforted him by saying that general business borrowing would soon pick up and then the banks would again come into their own. Two years went by and interest rates on commercial borrowing remained very low. Business demand for loans showed no signs of improvement. The bank now had a large part of its assets in Government bonds. These, however, returned only a small income and there was no turnover to bolster profits. Bank earning power was at a low ebb.

Then one day my banker friend was told to appear at a meeting in the head office. A plan for increasing the bank's earnings was under discussion. He appeared and received the shock of his life when he learned that the new magic earnings stimulant was to be a "personal loan department." Banking management had capitulated to the gauntlet thrown down by the credit and finance companies. The old standards of banking morals were being pushed aside by the trend of the times. They were being engulfed in the old sea of human cupidity. Consumer loans were not merely to be winked at—but were to be adopted by the bank and aggressively advocated.

The making of personal unsecured loans by commercial banks was new for my country banker friend. However, it was not new to some of the larger city banks, particularly in New York. Some large banks had realized a few years before that they themselves had been furnishing much of the money that was being used by the finance companies. The instalment loan companies had been borrowing large sums at very low rates from the banks and using these sums as working capital for their own loans at rates running from 11% to 16% per annum. The banks observed that the finance companies were prospering. Why should not the banker himself get some of the cream?

The real impetus to the small loan business on the part of the banks came from the period of poor bank earnings that followed the great expansion of Government debt beginning in 1933. Government deficit financing created a wealth of bank deposits and the banks were no longer called upon to create deposits by granting loans to business. The banks suffered acutely from a lack of high earning assets. Scruples about the desirability of granting consumer loans could be laid aside when they offered one avenue of escape from niggardly earnings.

Small loan, or personal loan, departments are now steadily increasing in the nation's banking system. They are a growing threat to the big credit and finance companies that have reaped such a golden harvest. I believe they will continue to cut into the finance companies' business. However, I am afraid that they will not make much headway against the real loan sharks. The loan sharks to which I refer are those small personal loan companies that prey on the needy and ignorant. They levy interest charges on their unfortunate victims not by the year, but by the month. They advertise loans at the low rate of 3% available on husband's and wife's signatures. No further collateral is necessary. The rate, to be sure, is $3 per hundred dollars borrowed; but it is due *monthly*, not yearly. As we have seen in previous discussions, the "low rate" thus actually exceeds an interest charge of 36% a year. Small wonder that the risk of losing the principal can be incurred by these vultures! The loan itself can soon be amortized on the company's books out of the usury charge. But the judgment remains against the poor debtor.

I predict that the personal loan departments of banks will make small progress in curing the evil of the "thirty-six percenters." The banks do investigate their small loan credit risks after a fashion. The patrons of the loan shark companies would hardly stand even the mild credit examination to which they would be subjected by the banks. However, I feel that the day is not far off when the public will take further action against these usurers.

HOW TO GO IN DEBT

How do these small loan departments of banks operate? In general the amount of the loan is limited to $500 or $1,000. The amount borrowed must be repaid within a period of twelve months. The interest charge is stated in terms of so many dollars per $100 borrowed per year. The loan is repaid on a monthly basis in equal instalments. No collateral is required and the signature is usually single, although in some banks the signatures of both husband and wife are required.

Some banks ask a fee of $1 before the loan is granted. This goes to defray the cost of a "credit report" on the applicant. Others pay for the credit report out of the general profits of the small loan department. When the loan is made, the interest charge is deducted in advance and the balance of the loan turned over to the applicant.

Why do not the banks express the interest charge in terms of percentage? Because the actual figure charged would be so high as to frighten the prospective customer. You see the loan is repaid in equal monthly instalments. If the borrower has paid his interest charge in advance he is really entitled to a rebate of interest each time he makes a payment. The bank makes no such rebate. Obviously, the interest collected in advance becomes a very high charge with relation to the declining amount of the loan still outstanding, say, at the end of ten months. Thus, the personal loan department advertises "loans at $6 per $100 per year." The borrower's immediate reaction is that he is receiving his loan at the comparatively low rate (for consumer loans) of 6% a year. Actually the percentage cost to him on his loan per year is closer to 12%!

Of course, this is no different from what happens to the instalment purchaser when he patronizes the finance company in order to buy a car or a refrigerator. Neither loaning agency, whether it be the bank or credit company, allows any rebate on the loan repayments as they are made. The true interest charge is a burden much heavier than realized. He who buys, not with cash, but with borrowed money, pays a heavy toll for the privilege of satisfying his desires without first exercising the fortitude that is necessary to saving in advance of purchasing.

Competition between banks and finance companies and between banks themselves should eventually bring a much lower cost to the consumer of borrowed money. Already some banks are quoting a rate of $5 per $100 instead of the customary $6 per $100. However, it is surprising how very little resistance there is among consumer borrowers to the high cost of loans of this nature.

LAMBS BEING SHORN

Recently, at a bank directors' meeting, the question came up as to what rate should be charged by the new Personal Loan Service that the bank was about to open. The directors (most of them had never purchased any household articles on an instalment basis in their lives) recommended to the officers of the bank a rate of $5 per $100. They figured that this low rate would attract business from the aggressive credit company in the town. The treasurer, however, reassured the directors that a rate of $6 per $100 would be just as easy to obtain and that much more profitable. His argument was that the borrowers would rather do business with the bank as it would be a novel experience for most of them and that $6 was the accepted "gentleman's charge" on such business. The directors were convinced, and $6 per $100 was the figure set. The treasurer's reasoning proved sound in the light of the bank's experience after the department was opened. The difference between $6 per $100 and the traditional 6% was never questioned by these borrowers!

Is it cheaper for an instalment purchaser to do business with the personal loan department of a bank than with a reputable credit company? My answer is "yes." However, the above experience of the bank opening a new small loan department makes me wonder if I am right when I say "yes." If the consumer borrower will not take the trouble to question the amount of the overcharge he is paying for the privilege of borrowing money, how can we teach him to buy real value? Therefore I make my answer "yes" to this problem with some misgivings and many reservations. The chief reservation is, of course, that the consumer purchaser should after borrowing the money take the time and effort to buy good merchandise at the right price. If he is to buy the first article offered for sale and pay the top price, he might just as well have bought from a high-pressure merchant with instalment-credit money.

ALL SO EASY!

To make this perfectly clear—it is the oft-told tale of frantic family financing: Tom Jones is in the market for a refrigerator. His wife has made up his mind that they need it, although they have not saved the purchase price. The lack of money is overcome by his wife's conviction (induced by advertisements that she has read) that a new mechanical refrigerator would pay its keep in the amount of food it would save from spoilage. They finally visit a refrigerator salesroom where the gentleman in charge enthralls them with his story. They are told not how much the refrigerator will cost, but how much they will have to pay monthly after making a small down payment. This is the standard story of how it starts.

It is all so easy. The salesman and the credit company that finances the refrigerator sale appear to be one and the same to Tom and his wife. Papers are signed, the small down payment is made, and Mrs. Jones goes home thinking about all the new gadgets that her refrigerator has compared with that of her neighbor. She thinks a little, too, of how much food this will save over her old chest. Now, Tom could still have bought this same refrigerator for much less than he paid under the above plan. He could have gone to the small loan department of a local bank and applied for a loan of, say, $200. A few days after making the application the bank would notify him whether they would grant his request. Then, armed with cash he could have done a little shopping for his refrigerator. He could have bought at a much lower price the equivalent of the one he purchased by doing some judicious inquiring. Even after paying the $6 per $100 interest rate charged by his local bank he should make a net saving of at least 10%. The fact is that Tom could have bought much cheaper if he had taken the time and made the effort. Would he? Well, some Toms would have—but probably more would not.

Buying an automobile by the use of small bank credit also introduces the possibility of some saving. This is particularly true if the prospective purchaser has no old car to turn in. The man who buys on the instalment plan through the bank small-loan-plan approaches the seller armed with cash. He does not have to rely on financing plans arranged "for his convenience" by the salesman. The seller need not know that business is being done on borrowed money. The buyer has the upper hand. With cash on hand it is often possible, *through intensive shopping,* to purchase a new car for a discount from the list price if the dealer is not taking in a used car in trade.

Of course, the car dealer makes a longer profit when the car he sells is put out through his own finance company. Therefore, he is not anxious to do business on a cash basis. However, with a standard make of car the careful buyer with cash can shop around until he finds some dealer ready to embrace the opportunity of making a quick cash sale. The car buyer who is trading in his old car can also save something if he has the cash ready before he approaches the seller. The saving here will be the amount of "forced insurance" that the finance company requires the time buyer to plaster on his new car. The buyer, by paying cash, can buy his own insurance. Again, after paying the $6 per $100 charge he should save at least 10%.

Incidentally, many of the bank personal loan departments insure the life of the borrower for the amount of the loan during the period it remains unpaid. For this service there is no extra charge to the borrower. The cost is assumed by the bank and is paid for out of the 10% to 12% interest rate realized by the bank on the money borrowed. I wonder if there is not something ironic in this life-insurance angle of the bank "consumer loan," especially when the banks must realize that a large part of their small loans are going to provide the borrower with nice new eighty-mile-an-hour cars?

Myriad are the uses to which the money borrowed from bank small-loan departments is put. The cost of a visit from the stork can thus be met in one fell swoop. A new set for the living room can be funded for a year's term. The cost of a new fur coat can be strung out over twelve months. It has made it possible for the unwilling saver to take advantage of bargains in linen and other household effects. On the other hand, before borrowing get a cash price from the stork!

All these advantages, and more too, were available for us and our fathers before the banks ceased to frown on "consumer loans." The small loan invention has merely reduced the burden on the profligate buyer. *It has made it less costly for him to be less thrifty.*

BANKER PERFORMS A SERVICE

Putting aside the technical question of whether a commercial bank should loan to support ultimate consumption, I see a real advantage in the growth of these bank small loan departments. Competition of the banks with the small credit companies, the big finance companies, and among themselves should gradually reduce the tremendous dead-weight interest burden that instalment buyers have been forced to bear in the past. You can readily see that the lower the interest charge falling on this type of purchase, the greater will be the purchasing power available for the articles that are being bought. Less for usury—more for production.

There is another favorable omen. A personal loan by the bank affords the instalment buyer some freedom of action in his shopping. Divorce of the loaning power from the seller should prove helpful in the long run. It should mean greater freedom of action for the buyer even if he is a dyed-in-the-wool instalment purchaser.

THRIFT SHOULD BE REWARDED

This trend toward direct bank financing of consumer loans is purely in the nature of an amelioration of a bad situation. The way to buy cheaply and economically is not by paying interest to a bank for the privilege of paying cash. The way to enjoy this privilege is to earn it. Make the banks pay you interest, not you pay interest to them, while you are earning your privilege of paying cash. Accumulate your cash buying power in a savings account and receive interest from the bank while you are doing it. That is what I meant when I said that "all the advantages, and more too, were available for us and our fathers" before bank consumer loans were invented.

You ask, "Isn't there *ever* any advantage in borrowing from a bank in order to pay cash?" My answer is that at the bottom of a depression, when goods are sacrificed at forced sales below their cost of production, there will be savings available that will undoubtedly be greater than the interest cost. Buyers at such times are however prudent men—and prudent men do not borrow to buy for consumption. One should never forget that the buyer who has cash saved can always buy at such times cheaper than the borrower by an amount equal to the interest charge paid by the borrower. *There is no substitute for thrift.*

Yes, the consumer should pay cash. But he should not borrow from the bank or any other place. Even though he saves fifty per cent on a purchase by careful buying, much of this saving will be eaten up in interest charges. The borrower buyer can never hope to buy as cheaply as the cash buyer, not so long as money costs money.

FROM BANKERS TO BUYERS

This leads to the question of whether the merchant should allow a discount of, say, 10% to the cash and carry buyer. We have seen how easy it is for a merchant-finance-company-tie-up to get a large part of the buying public to pay an overcharge of as much as 15% for the privilege of buying an article on "easy terms." In this case, however, the 15% represents an amount over and above what the cash customer would be asked to pay. As such it may be considered as a penalty on those who are unwilling to save first and take possession later. Even with those instalment buyers who borrow from the bank the charge for this service runs nearly 12% of the amount borrowed. In either case the extra charge borne by the borrower bears little relation to the distributor's cost of doing business.

Many distributors not only finance many of their customers by means of the old-fashioned open or charge account, but also by means of the so-called budget plan. The real difference between these two types is one of time, the length of time that the merchant carries the time buyer. The charge account is supposed to be cleared by the buyer at the first of the month that follows presentation of the bill. The budget plan is operated in many ways. In some cases it is a simple extension of the charge account to allow payment over a period of, say, three months. In others the cost of the article is frankly increased to allow for the carrying charge over the period of time payments.

ADVICE TO DEPARTMENT STORES

I have no bone to pick with merchandisers who add 10% or more to the price of an article when it is sold on a time payment plan—except when the charge is probably excessive. In fact, I am glad to see such a merchant recognizes, in principle at least, that the time, and not the cash buyer, should be penalized. (Of course, I feel that such a merchant is not a distributor of merchandise, but an operator of a little finance business all his own.) My appeal is that this same principle be recognized by merchants who do not overload their prices with this overcharge but who do a large credit business. I have especially in mind the department stores.

Yet, it is common practice for department stores to make no distinction between the cash buyer and the credit buyer. The public has been educated to believe that there is no virtue in the cash purchase. The distributor's attitude has been to establish the cost of distributing a lot of goods first and then sell the remainder of the lot at "sales" or in "bargain basements." Their attitude is, those who want to buy cheaply can afford to wait for these sales. Even at the sales the cash buyer who carries his purchase with him pays as much for his article as Mrs. Charge who never pays her bill until the third dunning and who rarely suffers the discomfort of carrying home her package. It is not difficult to figure out which of the above two buyers showed the distributor the larger profit per sale.

The fact is that the cash buyer who lugs off his parcel does not put the distributor to the same expense as the charge-account buyer who habitually makes use of the store's delivery and other services. Such practices on the part of the department stores may be good merchandising from their point of view, but I say that they do not give the cash buyer a break!

REWARDING THE INDUSTRIOUS

What about your own recent experience with cash and carry purchases vs. charge purchases in your own favorite department store? Perhaps you bought a pair of gloves at M's where you have a charge account.

You had them sent out. On arrival you decided that you did not need them. You mailed them back to M's with the request that your account be credited the amount of the glove charge. You received a courteous letter acknowledging receipt of the gloves and advice that the charge had been deducted from your account. No red tape—the case was quickly settled.

A few days later you were attracted to a handkerchief sale at X's department store. You went in and bought a dozen for cash. After looking them over at home you decided that you had been a little too optimistic and that half a dozen would have been sufficient. The next day you went back to X's to return half of your purchase. You explained the situation to the clerk from whom you made the purchase. He referred you to the floor walker. He sent you to the refund desk. There the gentleman informed you coldly that he would give you a credit slip in the amount of the refund. You might use this to buy anything in the store to the amount of the refund. Perhaps you fought on until you got the cash. Perhaps you decided it was not worth the effort. Who said the cash buyer got the breaks?

INSIST ON A DISCOUNT

The cash and carry buyer should insist on a discount when purchasing from distributors who do a general credit business. This discount should run from 5% to 10%. If you do not get a reduction from the price asked the credit buyer, you are only helping to carry the cost of doing business inefficiently on credit.

Actual losses are not a large part of this cost—they average well under 1% of gross sales. The cost of carrying slow accounts and of the abuses which have grown up out of the credit business is what makes up this 10%. I believe that the cash buyer should be able, therefore, to save this 10% in addition to the 10% finance charges which the instalment buyer pays. This should make a total savings of about 20%.

The cash and carry buyer saves the distributor credit loss, interest charges, delivery costs, and other expenses. In addition he furnishes the business with immediate working capital. These savings vary with the establishment but in many cases can run as high as 10%. Certainly the cash buyer is entitled to a discount. I believe such a discount will come as a natural result of the abuse of the instalment-plan business. Only by merchants frankly giving such a discount can they get back *on a cash or thirty days business basis*. Today many of these merchants are headed for a precipice.

CHAPTER ELEVEN

Our Government Is Running on "Instalments"

"Every child comes into the world endowed with liberty, opportunity and a share of the federal debt. The real white man's burden is debt."—*Stone*

It may seem a far cry from the ordinary run-of-the-mine instalment purchase to the question whether Uncle Sam is also a guilty party? Is Uncle Sam doing on a huge scale essentially what Mr. Brown does when he buys a new town sedan for so much cash down and for so much per month? But is this such a stretch of the imagination after all? When all is said and done instalment purchasing is the mortgaging of the future. Just as Esau of old sold his birthright for a mess of pottage, so thousands are plunging into debt —are mortgaging their futures—to satisfy a present whim. Already we have examined the plight of the family which after listening to a high-pressure salesman feels that life would not be worth living without the coveted article. Such a family is cajoled into gambling with the future by paying for only a small part of the glittering bauble and signing a series of notes for the balance. These notes may run for as long as eighteen months or more, title to the goods being withheld until the last note shall have been paid.

As we asked before, how can any bread-winner know positively that he will be able to make all those "easy" payments? Troubles, as the philosopher observes, have a way of coming not singly but in battalions. After several payments have been missed an agent from the finance company takes possession of the "pride and joy." Even that is not all, for the finance company may be unable to sell the goods for enough to pay fully for the balance due. So the wretched victim may be sued for the balance plus costs—an unexpected headache. Not only has the merchandise been lost, together with all the money paid in, but the defendant has to pinch and squeeze to pay for the judgment against him. Such a sufferer finally emerges from this baptism convinced of the folly of instalment buying. He is a chastened and wiser man.

UNCLE SAM A LEADER IN INSTALMENT BUYING

What have the humble citizen's instalment troubles got to do with Uncle Sam? Obviously, there is no direct connection. However, digging down we find the same principle involved in the relatively peewee instalment purchase of the private individual and the record-breaking spending of Uncle Sam. In both cases things are bought which are to be paid for in the future. In the final analysis there is no basic difference between instalment buying of an individual and the Government's spending far beyond its income. Both result in mortgaging the future.

Fundamental and all-powerful economic laws make no distinction between the two parties. The ultimate results are the same. Everyone recognizes that an individual cannot indefinitely spend more than he receives without going bankrupt. Many apparently think, however, that a Government can continue to spend more than it receives without a day of reckoning. The reason for this illusion is that the individual goes bankrupt quickly, whereas the tremendous resources of the Government enable it to delay the fatal day. The United States Government is not only running on an instalment basis, but it is a leader in the field. This is also true of most state and local governments. Uncle Sam is setting a fast—yes, a ruinous pace in spending far beyond his means.

GOVERNMENT'S SPENDING ORGY

Let us turn the spotlight for a moment upon the Government's spending activities and see what is going on. Just where does this country stand and where are we heading as regards this matter of spending and debt? In the early days of this country the Federal Government, with relatively few lapses, followed a conservative financial policy. Before 1932, Government spending was thrifty and for the most part careful and sane. Wasteful orgies were the exception not the rule and such sprees were relatively short-lived. Up to then, except in war times, Uncle Sam pursued the straight and narrow financial path. National debt was formerly regarded with horror and every effort was made to keep it down to low levels. When it rose, because of war, our statesmen subsequently adopted as quickly as possible a program of debt reduction. It was unthinkable that in times of peace we should have year after year a Federal budget which permitted spending far above total receipts.

Since 1933 sane spending and sound financial policies, as measured by standards of former years, have been thrown overboard. With few notable exceptions our politicians have vied with each other in spending our money. The depression brought with it a crisis which they believed necessitated extraordinary expenditures for relief and reconstruction. However, like hogs in a trough, the professional politicians seized the opportunity to spend money on an unheard of and undreamed of scale.

We have seen Government bureaus wax fat and politicians build powerful political machines fed by the people's money. When has there been such appalling waste and such extravagance in the history of this or any other country? Uncle Sam has been buying on the "instalment plan" with a vengeance. The worst of it is that we can discern few signs of any real checking of this spending orgy. The "morning after" will come just as surely as day follows night. It will give this country of ours a headache which will shake it to the tips of its toes.

RISING PUBLIC DEBT APPALLING

To be more specific what do the records show? Total expenditures of the Federal Government from the days of Washington to Wilson—a period of 124 years from 1789 to 1913—reached $24,521,843,000.

The total Federal Government debt in 1913 stood at
$1,193,047,745. That is a record of which all Ameri-
cans may well be proud. It would be fine if we could
stop there but unfortunately we must turn the page.
What do we find? Federal Government expenditures
of the New Deal Administration from June 30, 1934,
through June 30, 1937, reached the unbelievable total
of $31,465,832,056. In those four years, President
Franklin D. Roosevelt spent about 28% more than
was spent during the first 124 years of the country.
To show for all this we had a total Federal debt of
$36,424,614,000 on June 30, 1937.[1] This is an increase
of over 60% above the $22,538,673,164 debt on June
30, 1933—about four months after President Roosevelt
took over the reins.

No genial smile can laugh off Federal debt; it is
something which threatens the whole national economy. This debt should cause all voters, having an atom
of sense left, to place in Washington Congressmen who
will halt this spending orgy. The instalment-purchase
policy which Uncle Sam follows leads straight to national ruin, to a political and social upheaval. It is
not a pleasant picture but it should be faced squarely
by every man, woman, and child. We are placing a
mountainous mortgage on our future, a crushing load
on our children. Unlike an individual, there is no restriction on Uncle Sam when he goes on a spending
spree—except an aroused public opinion.

[1] Early in 1938, the total Federal debt had reached more than
$37,400,000,000.

Not only is the Federal Government plunging ever deeper into the morass of debt, but the states are following the lead of Washington. The rise in state debts has also been very rapid. From 1870 to 1912 the net increase was $341,000,000, or only 6%. From 1912 to 1922, however, the net debt of the states soared 205%. Casting all caution to the winds, they went on a spending orgy which broke all previous records. Of course the war played a large part in increasing state expenditures; but from 1922 to 1932 the total debt of the forty-eight states was boosted another 34%. The records show that the state debts multiplied almost ten times in the twenty-five years following 1912, reaching $3,186,043,409 on June 30, 1937. This compared with a debt of $2,372,041,765 on June 30, 1930 —only seven years previous. The total gross state debt is broken down as follows: [2]

	Amount	Per Cent of Total
Highway, bridge, etc.	$1,444,528,432	45.34
General improvement	624,009,740	19.58
Revenue-producing enterprises	479,321,977	15.04
Veterans' bonus, etc.[3]	189,878,760	5.96
Deficit funding	114,002,200	3.57
Relief	334,294,600	10.49
Total	$3,186,043,409	100.00

[2] Table from "Resources and Debts of the Forty-Eight States, 1937," by Edna Trull, by courtesy of the publisher, Dun & Bradstreet, Inc.

[3] One large group of bonds issued exclusively to benefit veterans is included with the revenue enterprises. If this is added to the figures shown for veterans, the latter becomes 8.6% of the total.

202 THE FOLLY OF INSTALMENT BUYING

The states have acquired the pernicious habit of living on the instalment plan. This has been the inevitable result of the example set by Washington together with the intense spending mania which characterizes these "modern" times. The whole nation aspires to an ever higher standard of living which is putting an ever-increasing strain on us all. It is plunging the nation headlong into debt at a fearful pace. There will be loud wails and gnashing of teeth when the settlement day finally arrives.

Would that we could stop here in our probing into the subject of Government spending and the rising debt. Turning to municipalities and local governments, which number about 175,000, we find that they also are living on the instalment plan. Some of our cities have gone one better than Uncle Sam himself, though of course their expenditures are small change in comparison with his vast disbursements. Washington officials coming from the large cities had been trained in the art of spending the people's money and organizing political machines. Cities are for the professional politician a training school where he learns the ropes preparatory to graduating into state and national affairs.

These local politicians certainly know how to spend. Local debt has mounted higher and higher until many cities are staggering under a crushing load. Local taxes have risen so high that it often becomes advisable for a manufacturer to move to another city. Municipal bonds as a whole are under a cloud. Investors have learned to their sorrow that cities can and do default. Total local net tax-supported debt was estimated to be about $12,000,000,000 on June 30, 1937, and still rising. Instead of signing notes to be paid over a year or eighteen months, as does the individual instalment buyer, the city, state, and Federal Governments issue bonds and other forms of indebtedness. In the final show-down these securities are no more than I.O.U.'s and are worth no more than the ability or the willingness of the people to pay. Some of these local bonds are not worth the paper on which they are printed. That brings me to another point for consideration— the security and rights of the seller or lender.

WHAT SECURITY?

When an individual is unable to continue his instalment payments, the finance company exercises its rights and acts to protect itself. After several letters of warning, if no payments are forthcoming, the property which was "sold" is repossessed. Here is where there is a basic difference between the humble citizen's notes and Uncle Sam's bonds. It is, of course, elementary that the safety valve of instalment selling is the right and power to foreclose,—that is, to repossess. However, should the Federal Government decide to default on any of its bonds, what then? The holder of the defaulted bond indeed would be in trouble and would have every reason to be downhearted.

What are the rights of a government bondholder? What can he do? In the days of old—when kings were

kings they were the law—they and they alone decided
what was right and wrong. They could not be judged
for "the King could do no wrong." Hence, came the
common law that the Government cannot be sued unless it specifically gives permission to do so. This is
where the Court of Claims enters the picture. It has
authority to hear and decide all claims against the
Federal Government which are allowed. This includes
acts of Congress, regulations of the executive department, or any contract entered into by the Government.

WHEN UNCLE SAM DEFAULTS

The holder of defaulted bonds, therefore, has no
such protective rights as exist in the ordinary instalment sale. There is no mortgage involved but merely
the promise of Uncle Sam to pay on a certain day.
The Government bond is in fact a debenture bond,
an I.O.U. There can be no foreclosure or repossession.
In seeking to recover, the unfortunate defaulted bondholder would probably be forced to fight a long court
battle. What would the Court finally decide? Still
fresh in our memories are the famous "gold clause"
battles of 1934-1936 when Uncle Sam refused to live
up to his promise to pay in the yellow metal. An individual or company would be jailed for such a breach
of good faith. If Uncle Sam does not choose to pay,
it's just too bad for the bondholder.

States and local governments cannot be sued under
the law unless due provision has been made for same.
As a matter of fact, however, many states have laws

permitting suits for damages in certain instances. Assuming the state permits suit in case of default on its bonds and those of localities within its borders, the holder of the defaulted state or municipal bond is faced with a long drawn out legal process. The one advantage of bonds issued by the Federal Government is that said Government can—as a last resort—print money to pay them. No state, municipality or corporation can do this.

Even where the Federal, State or Municipal Government bonds might actually be for a bridge, tunnel or some other specific public work, there is no opportunity to foreclose. In this connection you will recall the difficulties experienced in the depression in foreclosing private properties, especially farms. There was no question as to the right to foreclosure; such violence arose that the creditors did not dare to foreclose. That thing called public opinion cannot be overlooked. It certainly would be strong against any who might try to exercise his right to foreclose on a bridge, tunnel or other public work. So we see that our government financing has all the worst features of instalment buying with few of the safeguards or advantages. It is largely a case of "try to recover" should the Federal, state or local governments default on any of their bonds.

THE DOWN-PAYMENT PITFALL

In addition to this matter of security another vital feature of instalment sales is the down payment. How the salesman uses it in his arguments to get you to sign on the dotted line! For only a few dollars paid down you can buy a new fur coat, a refrigerator or a new bed-room set. Back of this down payment is the theory of its protection to the seller. The amount of the down payment varies substantially depending on several factors. In the case of merchandise with a high repossession value, the required down payment demanded can be made relatively small both as to amount and to the percentage of the total.

Instalment terms stiffen as the repossession value of the product decreases. Thus an oil burner, for example, is estimated to have a comparatively long life. It retains its value to a greater degree than, say, a fur coat. Consequently an oil burner can more safely be sold, so the theory runs, for a comparatively small down payment. On the other hand, the fur coat has a much shorter life than the oil burner; while in addition style changes might make it out of fashion in a year or two. Hence, the down payment on the fur coat should represent a larger percentage of the garment's list price. Thus we see the importance of the varying cash down payments in safeguarding and in controlling instalment sales.

But what about Uncle Sam? Does he make any down payment in his "instalment buying"? Again let us turn to the records. Briefly, statistics show that total receipts for the year ending June 30, 1937, reached $5,293,840,237. This compared with $4,033,250,225 in the boom year of 1929. However, Uncle Sam's total expenditures for the fiscal year of 1937 reached $8,105,-158,547! These were second only to the previous year's all time high for expenditures in peace times. This plunged the country further into debt to the tune of $2,646,070,000. It is obvious from the foregoing figures that the Government paid very little down payments in its spending spree.

Total public-work expenditures alone for 1937 slightly exceeded $3,000,000,000. Figuring roughly Uncle Sam's operating expenses at about $5,000,000,-000, leaves only about $100,000,000 as the "cash payment." The Federal Government has been spending our heritage at a terrific rate. This by comparison makes the ordinary instalment purchase appear ultra-conservative. Federal down payments are grossly inadequate from a conservative viewpoint. There is yet another sharp difference between Government "instalment buying" and that of the individual. This is that, unfortunately, there are none to regulate what Uncle Sam does. There are no fixed rules to keep Government spending within bounds, under proper control. In other words, in "buying on time" the Government can pay little, or no down payment, as it chooses.

DECEPTIVE INTEREST RATES

In instalment purchasing the rate of interest is still another method of limiting the risks of the seller and keeping sales under control. By this we refer not merely to the nominal rate being charged, but to the real and effective rate. Almost everyone realizes that "you only have to pay 6%" actually means that the buyer is being charged about 12%. The consumer, however, is willing to pay this exorbitant rate for the privilege of having the electric refrigerator, the automobile or the living-room furniture. The seller raises the instalment charge to halt excessive buying, and lowers the rate of interest to stimulate sales when they are at low ebb. The rate of interest is, therefore, one of the factors which are supposed to act as an automatic brake on the private instalment business.

But let us consider this matter of interest rates in connection with the Government's policy of "instalment buying." Normally, as the total loan expands and the risk is thereby increased, it is to be expected that the interest rate would rise. Conversely, rates are supposed to decrease as total loans contract. Low interest rates have in the past signified a relatively low level of loans—or debts. Therefore, the present extremely low interest rates on Government notes and bonds is very misleading. Far from reflecting the rapidly pyramiding public debt, they would point to a low and decreasing total debt. How deceptive the current interest rates are in "hiding" Uncle Sam's true financial condition and trend!

Interest rates on Federal notes and bonds are deceptive in another way. Do not overlook the fact that they are granted tax-exempt concessions. For this reason also I contend that the nominal rate of interest paid by the Government on its "instalment purchases" is in reality not even nominal; it is fictitious! The true rate is obscured and distorted. The interest rate on Government notes and bonds does not even act as a crude control of Uncle Sam's "instalment" orgy. So we can only conclude that when the Government has embarked on the treacherous waters of "easy-payment plans," it becomes an easy victim for the rapids and the whirlpools. Uncle Sam's surrender to instalment temptations is unrestrained and unrestricted by even the partial precautions which surround the individual buyer. Only thoroughly aroused public opinion can effectively halt the Government's spending spree. Can this happen before it is too late? That is a question.

THE PUBLIC IS ASLEEP

One of the primary reasons for the apathy which characterizes the general public as regards Uncle Sam's spending, is ignorance of the rank and file regarding the true state of affairs. In turn the chief reason for this ignorance and lack of concern as to what is going on is the fact that a very small proportion of the people are taxed directly. The long-suffering public pays numerous hidden taxes, during the course of the year; although for a single individual these are in small sums. Very often these taxes are included in the price of the thing purchased. For example, gasoline is one of the commodities which has long been a favorite tax source for politicians. State taxes range from 2c to as high as 7c per gallon, while in addition the Federal Government and some cities also collect taxes thereon. The consumer pays with little protest. Why? Largely because the price to him is so much per gallon which includes all these sundry taxes. If the oil companies were to sell by having the consumer pay so much for the gasoline and so much additional for the taxes, a wave of public protest might arise. Then gasoline taxes would be reduced to fair and reasonable levels.

WHO WILL PAY THE BILLS?

The public is not yet really tax conscious, although there are signs that more people are becoming so. The masses have not yet been hard hit in the pocketbook by direct Federal and State taxes. The politicians have been careful to avoid that. Take the matter of income taxes which are paid to the Federal Government. For the year ending June 30, 1937, total individual income taxes collected by Uncle Sam reached $1,091,740,746.42—an increase of 62% over 1936 and the largest since 1930. Individual income taxes represented 23½% of the total receipts of the Federal Government during the fiscal year ending June 30, 1937.

Just who paid this huge tax? There were 6,735,454 income returns filed in 1937 and of these it is estimated that only 4,500,000 actually dug down into their pockets to pay the tax. Stated another way only about 10% of the voters in this country have to file income returns and only about 7% pay any income tax. The income tax burden falls heavily on the shoulders of but a small fraction of the voters—they are still hearsay to about 93%. This is politically sound, for the man in the street pays nothing and feels elated over "soaking the rich."

The time is fast approaching, however, when the tax gatherers will be forced to lower the tax base. Indications are that tax rebellion will gather force. By

1940 or 1942 many more voters will be forced to file income returns and will have to contribute to the expenses of the Federal Government. This inevitable broadening of the tax base should definitely tend to make numerous voters more tax conscious. It may even thoroughly arouse the public;—the sleeping dog may awaken and go for the political spenders with teeth bared.

If, as and when the public is really stirred,—when the people finally have to pay as they surely will— then Federal expenditures will be radically cut. It will be hard on the fat politician. Portly bureaucrats will grow thin; but Uncle Sam will again get back to earth and live within his income. He will have to pay for his sins,—for ruthlessly wasting national resources and plunging this country into such tremendous indebtedness. The public will become more tax conscious. This should check the Government's "instalment buying" spree,—we hope before it is too late. Otherwise there will ultimately be radical inflation, final collapse and chaos.

MAKING IT "EASIER" TO PAY

One of the dangers of instalment purchases has been the tendency in certain periods to lengthen the time of payments. Notes used to be limited to a period of one year; but now loans are made for two or three years. Salesmen and advertisers urge us to buy the oil burner at so much down and "three years to pay." Lengthening of the time in which loans are to be paid is making it easier for Mr. and Mrs. Consumer to overload themselves. It encourages buying many things they really do not need. By loading themselves to the breaking point it becomes increasingly difficult, and too often impossible, for them to continue payments.

What is more, pinching to dig up the necessary money to meet notes coming due, results in lowering appreciably the instalment buyer's effective purchasing power. Mr. and Mrs. Consumer thus learn that they cannot eat their cake and have it too. This means deferred buying of many items in the months following the instalment purchases. This hurts both the consumer and the seller. Buying on time tends to boost sales unduly when business is moving along at a brisk pace and everyone is optimistic. It leads to over-expansion, thereby helping to pave the way for a slump in sales and business later on.

This is true of lengthening the time of payments for the ordinary instalment purchase. It is also true of the Government's purchasing "on time." There are strong arguments for heavy Federal spending to start the ball rolling when times are hard. Within reason, priming the pump may be justified. When business gets going under its own steam, pump-priming and nursing are unnecessary. Continued Government spending, far in excess of income, then accentuates the bulge in activity and creates maladjustments. When business is rising, the Government should cut down on spending. It should put its financial house in order, live within its income, reduce its indebtedness. What will happen when the Government has to spend tremendous sums in the next major depression to help pull us out of the swamp of the next depression if it fails now to balance the budget and materially reduce the national debt?

Government borrowing for periods of ten or twenty years is bad enough. However, perhaps the most sinister and dangerous form of Government financing, as regards its ultimate possibilities, is the so-called temporary notes with indefinite and unknown final maturity. In practice, these notes are merely refunded with no attempt to liquidate them in any serious way, although allowance is made for the provisions for sinking funds in the Federal budget. These debts, therefore, can go on almost endlessly. They constitute an instalment purchase so to speak in which the notes are allowed to run for an indefinite period. Sound financial standards in instalment selling make such a system unthinkable and impossible. Yet that is precisely what Uncle Sam is doing,—another basic difference in the Government's "time-payment program" from that of industry and commerce.

GOVERNMENT THE HORRIBLE EXAMPLE

Probably one of the most subtly dangerous, insidious results of the Government's "instalment buying" —its grossly extravagant spending far in excess of income—is the moral effect upon the people. Uncle Sam sets a horrible example in wasteful spending which should make our forefathers turn over in their graves. The homely virtues of the hardy and courageous people who dared their all to hew this country out of the wilderness have been forgotten. The streamlined politician of these latter days sneers at thrift as something out of date. It was all right in the horse and buggy days when people were not so smart—or were they smarter? Our forefathers with all those homely virtues, now so commonly ridiculed, did a pretty fair job in developing this country of ours.

The crash and depression which followed 1929 apparently failed to deflate some who are preaching the false doctrines of "easy" living. "Live today," they chant, "for tomorrow you may die—there may be another war or something else to turn the world upside down. So live on, spend, enjoy while you may and take no serious thought for the morrow. The Social Security funds will provide." With the Government taking the lead in this mad spending orgy, it is no wonder that the masses follow and likewise spend.

Many are extending their time purchases for merchandise far above levels of reason or safety. They are being encouraged to do so by the Government's extravagance and by the prevailing philosophy of dishonesty. These people are riding for a terrific fall and so is this country. The hand-writing is on the wall. We must have the honesty to face the facts—no matter how disagreeable and unpleasant. We should act. Unless we clean house and halt this wild, uncontrolled spending orgy, this worship of the god of "easy living" will spell the ultimate doom of our democracy. Reckless instalment buying by Uncle Sam may pave the way for *real trouble,* an economic and social upheaval which will end these United States as we know them.

CHAPTER TWELVE

SOME MORE IMPORTANT CONSIDERATIONS

"He looks the whole world in the face for he owes not
any man."—*Longfellow*

I have always enjoyed reading Chinese philosophy.
Notwithstanding China's defeats, both past and present, the Chinese nation survives. China perhaps has
the oldest history of any existing nation. It is true
that "the ways of the Chinese are peculiar" and, at
times, inscrutable. Yet, these very customs which seem
odd to us may be their strength.

Chinese sayings and proverbs have greatly interested
me. Much of the philosophy contained in the Bible
came from or through China. I am reminded by my
friends of one of these Chinese proverbs as I start to
write this chapter. It is this: *"When riding a lion, it
is very dangerous to dismount."* The previous chapters
of this book show clearly that the instalment industry
is a lion. My friends are telling me that it is here to
stay; that it would be dangerous to curtail it and I
had better forget it and think of something cheerful.
I, however, am also reminded of another Chinese prov-
erb which is this: *"For a kite to rise, it must be flown
against the wind."* Therefore, notwithstanding the un-
popularity of combating this great instalment industry,

I will complete the story. At least, I hope my "pay-as-you-go" kite will rise enough to be seen by a million readers.

As long as people are foolish there will be physical illnesses. No legislation or medical discovery can prevent their occurrence. Only as people acquire self-control, along with their knowledge, will the nation become truly healthier. In the same way, as long as people are selfish, there will be business depressions. No legislation or statistical chart can prevent their re-currence. Only as people acquire character and intelligence, will the nation improve economically.

SPIRITUAL PROBLEMS

Self-control and patience, like faith and courage, are spiritual qualities. They cannot be learned or pur-chased. They come only as our motives and ambitions are changed by a spiritual rebirth. Hence, in the last analysis, the instalment problem is very deep-rooted. Its solution rests with the spiritual state of the nation, the people's willingness to wait, save, sacrifice and struggle. The instalment problem may almost be com-pared to the liquor or vice problem. Only as our "hearts" are changed, will its evils gradually be elim-inated en masse.

There is sure to be another severe business depres-sion some day. With it will come unemployment, fall-ing prices, business failures, home foreclosures and worse disasters than were seen from 1930 to 1935. Such a depression always has followed a period of excep-tionally good times. It does not directly follow a period of hard times. Night follows day; rain follows sunshine. There cannot be valleys without hills; but where there are valleys, hills may always be found. Usually these hills are rocky and barren.

During the years ahead, purchases on instalments are destined to be an important factor in creating the boom times and hence in bringing on hard times. When people are content to buy normally for cash, then there is little danger in the merchandise situation. When, however, people anticipate their future needs by instalment purchases, then normal times become good times. (Unfortunately, only exceptionally good times or boom times are called "good" by most people.) When people get their advance needs temporarily satisfied they stop buying. This creates hard times, which are those periods when people do not buy even for their current needs.

The above principle applies to buying both stocks and commodities. No stock-exchange boom or panic ever occurred when all stocks and bonds had been bought and paid for in cash. It is buying these securities on margins or instalments which causes the abnormal boom which carries prices too high. When investors have satisfied both their present needs and anticipated their future needs, they stop buying more securities. Stock prices then fall as there are no buyers.

Surely the same principle applies to buying automobiles, refrigerators, fur coats and every other commodity which is sold on instalments. One cannot use an unlimited amount of these things. Instalment buying helps business *today;* but today's instalment buying must of necessity hurt business *tomorrow.* The Law of Action and Reaction is as fundamental as the Law of Gravitation. To ignore its reality, results in trouble, disappointment and loss.

This means that the next major depression may not be of Wall Street origin, but rather of Main Street origin. People were so burned by the Florida boom in 1922-1926 that they—*for a time*—learned another important lesson. People were so burned by the Wall Street debacle of 1929-1932, that they—*for a time*—learned another important lesson. People, however, up to 1938, had not learned that the indiscriminate buying of automobiles on instalments can cause a panic as well as the indiscriminate buying of real estate or stocks.

For this reason, I am especially fearful of the political reverberations of the next depression. Many more people will both directly and indirectly then be hurt. This means that more people then will lose property and more people then will be thrown out of work. I say this because so many more people buy merchandise on instalments than ever bought either real estate or stocks. Hence, beware of the trouble which some day is coming to us. It may be so severe as to bring on revolution.

INSTALMENT BUYING DEEP-ROOTED

There is a tendency to think of instalment buying as a new invention. It certainly has greatly increased since the World War. It rose to great heights in 1926-

1929 and again in 1935-1938. These past "booms" in instalment business will be followed by even greater surges in years to come. It is inherent in human nature to buy on instalments as it is to use liquor or to gamble.

In a previous chapter I traced the history of the instalment business. It started years ago in a very humble but natural manner. Hence, although the industry appears young, it also is old. The cream of the industry can easily be skimmed or checked. Instalment buying in some form will never be suppressed. Furthermore, I am not so sure that it should be wholly eliminated. Nothing is wholly right or wholly wrong. Circumstances still alter cases.

As a rule, things and practices are not harmful until they are commercialized. For instance, wine, beer and spirits have been brewed at home for thousands of years. Only comparatively recently has their sale been exploited. It was when the breweries began financing the corner saloons that trouble brewed, which brought on the downfall of both. This same principle applies to the theater, cards, short stories, dancing and other things. These may be good in themselves, but are misused and abused through commercial exploitation.

Instalment selling has been exploited and abused by the finance companies. These companies acquire large capital by selling stock to the public. This capital they loan by "purchasing" notes given by individuals in connection with the buying of automobiles, refrigerators and other merchandise. The dealers endorse the notes and thus get the money from the finance company. These companies have elaborate organizations for collecting the money. Naturally, the cost is heavy. This cost falls upon the ultimate consumers of the goods.

There are a very large number of finance companies varying in size and nature of work. Moreover, I am not including herewith the Morris Banks and the various personal loan companies which have always existed. These latter loan to individuals money to keep up their instalment payments to the finance companies. The finance companies do business on a wholesale scale. Their total of operations is very large. In fact, the Federal Department of Justice is said to be making a study of these companies with the idea of prosecuting them under the Sherman Anti-Trust Act.

Many feel that finance companies are only glorified pawnshops. In some ways they are worse than pawnshops. They entice a person to borrow even *before* he gets into trouble. Hence, when real trouble comes, his property and income have been so mortgaged that he has no reserve. This of itself is a very serious situation. Thus one becomes addicted to instalment buying as he would become addicted to liquor or gambling or any other vice. The only way to avoid the dangers of instalment buying is to quit it entirely, NOW.

One of the chief causes of labor troubles has been instalment buying. I truly believe that instalment buying was an important factor in creating John L. Lewis and his C.I.O. Most families were happy with their wages before instalment buying became the fashion. They did not have all they wanted, but they had plenty to eat, wear and a place to sleep. Wages were small but it was possible for one to secure work all the year. This gave people an income upon which they could depend.

The purchase of cars, refrigerators, radios, fur coats, etc., by these families on instalments had two bad effects, viz.: (1) Such purchases magnified the ups and downs of the business cycle and thus made work less steady. There were more shut-downs and off days. (2) Such instalment purchases took so much of the weekly wage to make the monthly instalment payments that there really was not enough left to pay for the needed food, clothing and shelter. Instead of urging those families to quit buying merchandise on instalments, the labor organizations demanded in their behalf more pay. They usually got the increase in hourly wages; but with it went fewer days of work. The net result at the end of the year was nil.

INSTALMENT SALES INCREASE PRICES

Probably these finance companies have more salesmen indirectly working for them than has any other industry. I say this because every salesman of automobiles, every salesman of refrigerators, and every salesman of other merchandise, sold on instalments, is actually a salesman for the finance company. No wonder that the business of these finance companies has grown by leaps and bounds. From a similar standpoint the newspapers have been a great aid to instalment selling. Formerly the department stores were content to advertise their goods for cash. Then they began to open credit accounts; but later they openly advertised that their goods could be bought upon instalments. A typical advertisement is of an electric refrigerator which sells for $130 and may be obtained by paying only $5 down and $5 per month.

It is thus seen that almost everyone is engaged in this serious traffic: manufacturers, railroads, jobbers, merchants, salesmen, newspapers, magazines and now the radio broadcasting companies. Turn on your radio any night and note how the public is being urged, coaxed, bullied and frightened into buying things on instalments. The entire practice is dangerous and vicious. It seems as if the best brains of the nation were engaged in erecting a house of cards only to be knocked down later.

For many years I have always had one grandchild in the "block age." I mean at that time of life, from three to four years old, when a child enjoys playing with wooden blocks. We make houses and fences and all kinds of things of blocks. What I enjoy most, however, is to aid in building a "tower." We place one block upon another to see how many we can place in position before they all collapse. My record to date is four grandchildren and forty blocks! Each grandchild at some time asks this question: "Why do you let the blocks fall?"

Readers naturally say: "If instalment exploitation is so dangerous, why is it permitted?" The answer is contained in the fact that so many persons are interested in it. Instalment selling is the bull which American business has by the tail. It seems as if business cannot let go for fear the bull will turn and then— "good night!" The situation is deeply complicated. Everyone who has studied the problem knows it is very serious, but all fear to check it.

The Federal Government at times gets after the finance companies, but this is to force them to reduce their rates of interest and miscellaneous charges. No Washington Administration has ever dared to stop the business or even take effectual steps to check it. Politicians fear that any such campaign would result in a cessation of sales, followed by merchants failing, factories shutting down and millions of people being thrown out of employment. Yet, this very thing happens once in so often without any government interference. No legislation is necessary to prevent me from trying to pile more than forty blocks one upon another!

I am, however, certain that since the 1929-1935 depression instalment selling has been the greatest factor in causing the severe fluctuations in the business curve. These fluctuations formerly were caused by crop conditions, money rates and similar fundamentals. Gradually these seemed to balance one another. Or perhaps crops have been so diversified that a failure in one section results in increased prices in another, so that the nation as a whole does not suffer.

I am even more certain that the instalment industry has been a great factor in keeping people unhappy and dissatisfied. Not only has it forced labor to demand more money, in order both to pay the instalment dues and keep body and soul together, but the continual advertising of these instalment bargains has been bad. It has resulted in making the entire family economic Bolshevists. Father has hardly dared to bring home at night a newspaper for fear the advertisements would create a family row.

PLAYING WITH BLOCKS

Instalment selling, as now exploited by all these different interests, bears the same relation to general business as do blocks in building a child's tower. Instalment selling started with the home block. It was wise to urge people to buy homes and pay for them over a long term of years. This was followed by various plans to enable people to buy good securities on a partial-payment plan. Some of the companies promoting these plans were reliable; but others were not. When I was a boy about the only merchandise sold on partial payments were sets of books, especially encyclopedias. These were sold not by stores but by house-to-house canvassers. I remember there was great indignation among local merchants in my home city of Gloucester, Massachusetts, when a western stove manufacturer advertised to sell coal stoves on the partial-payment plan.

Beginning about 1900, other articles began to be advertised at "$5 down and $1 per month." Phonographs were one of the articles which were freely sold on instalments. Then followed motor cycles and various other things which could readily be recovered if the purchaser ceased his monthly payments. They were things which the neighbors would miss if the goods were taken back. *This last was very important.* Pride has been a great help in building up and protecting the instalment industry.

For many years the big merchandisers and large department stores did only a cash business. The instalment business was mostly being done by new and smaller concerns. After ten or fifteen years experience, it was seen, however, that the losses on these instalment sales were almost negligible. This especially was true when the sales were limited to rural districts. Furthermore, it was known that those who sold on instalments secured a better price and a better profit.

Certain magazines which had a large rural circulation specialized in this instalment advertising. The instalment business soon became a gold mine for these younger concerns. Finally, the big, established firms could no longer resist the trend. They decided to let down the bars. The great increase in the sales of certain large concerns which took place from 1922 to 1928 was largely due to their going into the instalment business.

Of course, this was almost fatal to many small concerns which had been reaping such a rich harvest. Some of these simply folded up and retired from the field. Others consolidated or sold out. A few kept on; but their "honey days" were over. From that time on the industry grew very rapidly. Each year more and more things were sold on instalments. Finally, the big automobile companies opened wide the flood gates, until over 70% of all cars were sold on partial payments.

Today it is possible to buy anything and everything on instalments. This applies from paint to put on your house, to a trip to Europe. Whether or not the thing sold is recoverable, seems to be no longer considered.

The sellers or the finance companies send the prospective purchaser an elaborate questionnaire in order to cull out the worst prospects. They are frightened by the questions, refuse to fill out the blank and drop out of the picture. Anyone who fills out and signs a questionnaire, however, is pretty certain to get the merchandise. Some companies may not even bother to read the answers or look up the references. They operate on the law of averages like an insurance company. They determine from "actuarial" figures what the percentage of loss under certain business conditions will be and merely add this to the price. They appear to do as well as the few concerns which have elaborate credit departments.

INSTALMENT SELLING AND THE PRICE LEVEL

A previous chapter shows clearly what instalment buying needlessly costs the public above the real price of the goods. Therefore, I need not elaborate on this point. In total, the cost must amount to an unnecessary billion dollars per year! In other words, if people would pay cash, they could save one billion dollars each year on the goods purchased as well as have a peaceful mind. *Although the great curse of the instalment business goes far deeper than the additional money cost involved,* I do wish to discuss in this chapter the effect of instalment buying on the general price level. In short, I believe that everyone is paying more for all goods owing to the instalment purchases of the few people who do not pay cash. This is a very important matter. It may be an important cause of the buyers' strikes which develop every so often during each business cycle.

All readers should be acquainted with the workings of inflation.[1] Inflation consists of manufacturing money. This changes the value of outstanding money unless there has been a corresponding increase in the country's real wealth. "Unless the intrinsic wealth of the country, in the terms of useful commodities such as farms, homes, factories, stores, railroads, steamships, public utilities and other forms of useful enterprise, is increased proportionately, inflation results in cheapening the value of the existing money which you have in your pocket or bank.

Changing the value of money is like changing the size of a quart measure or of a foot rule. By so doing, it is easy to increase the *number* of quarts or the *number* of feet; but there is no more milk for food or no more cloth for clothing. This is *very important for people* to realize as the politicians are always attempting to fool us by increasing the number of dollars without increasing the amount of food, clothing and shelter.

There are various ways to manufacture money. The rankest and frankest method is for the Government to

---

[1] For details see "If Inflation Comes" by Roger W. Babson. Frederick A. Stokes Company, 443 Fourth Avenue, New York City. 1937. $1.35 postpaid.

print it as was done in Germany some years ago. Then the Mark in terms of purchasing power dropped from 20 cents to $\dfrac{1}{100,000}$ of a cent or even less. This was accomplished simply by printing or manufacturing money faster than goods were manufactured. The process was started innocently, but the final result was terribly unfortunate to everyone.

Another way to manufacture money is for individuals to typewrite it, as was done in Florida from 1922 to 1926. A Government note is only a promise of the Government to pay "one dollar" on demand. A personal note is the promise of an individual to pay "one dollar" on demand. The main difference is the kind of paper and ink that is used. Now the instalment business requires the printing, typing and issuing of these personal notes. Their effect on the general price level, however, is as dangerous as if the Government issued them.

The above means that the actual amount of money in circulation in the United States increases proportionally to the instalment sales. Consequently, prices of all articles may increase as instalment sales increase. I say this because in reality Germany's collapse came about not because the Mark declined, *but rather because the price of goods increased*. People knew that the money was worth less, the more that was printed. Hence, they demanded more of this paper money for their goods.

Inflation always causes an increase in the price level. The manufacture of money in any form, or in any way, always causes an increase in prices unless there has been a corresponding increase in the nation's wealth. Therefore, the only remaining question is whether or not the instalment business does increase the nation's wealth proportionately to the increase in outstanding instalment paper. I answer this emphatically with a "No," notwithstanding the fact that 90% of the instalment paper is retired within three years.

CAPITAL OR CONSUMER GOODS

This brings us to a further discussion of the usefulness and length of life of the things purchased. No one would argue that the country is richer by selling U. S. citizens trips to Europe on instalments. Not only is the trip non-recoverable, in case of non-payment of the notes; but the money is being spent outside of the country. Never mind how much one may argue for the educational and cultural values of a European trip, the facts show that the United States is poorer, rather than richer, by such instalment sales.

On the other hand, the country is richer by selling U. S. citizens durable trucks to haul farm produce. Even in this case, however, we should consider both the life of the truck and also the value of certain existing railroad equipment which said truck sends to the junk pile. It is evident that the problem is very complicated as most articles sold on instalments come midway between the European trip group and the farmer's truck group.

But to continue this illustration for a moment more, think of a further complication. The farmer must buy and forever use up gasoline to operate the truck, while he himself had raised hay and oats to "operate" the horses which the truck displaced. Furthermore, the horses made manure which went back to and fed the soil. Therefore, it is very difficult not only to classify, but to analyze the ramifications of an instalment purchase.

The entire business structure is like a finely made watch. Each of us is only a minute cog of some wheel. Yet, we all must move together in the proper direction and at a proper rate of speed. The failure of any cog stops the watch. Some day our economic constitution may get acclimated to instalment purchases. Nature has a way of adjusting itself to almost anything. This adjustment has not yet taken place. Until it does, instalment selling will continue to be a serious factor in determining the course of the business cycle.

If all people did business on a cash basis and if no one borrowed money, I could visualize a great flattening out of the business curve. This would mean much steadied commodity prices, more stable employment conditions and more normal profits. The "feast and famine" economic program would be set aside for a normal program. The rapid changes in the business curve are what cause losses, unemployment and failures. The economic peaks and valleys are due to abnormally active business and high prices when people are *borrowing* to buy and build. This is followed by abnormally inactive business and low prices when people are forced to economize in order to pay up these loans. Hence, business swings from good times to bad times. Furthermore, the extent of the bad times is apt to be proportional to the intensity of the preceding period of prosperity.

Instalment buying is only a form of borrowing. It, therefore, is a very important factor in the business cycle. The invisibility of these instalment loans adds to their seriousness. The financial and business interests always know the outstanding bank loans and the loans to brokers. The loans of the large finance companies are now public; but no statistics are available as to the total outstanding instalment indebtedness of the country at any one time. Yet, these statistics are very necessary before future business conditions can be forecast with a fair degree of accuracy.

Let me here add that the instalment business has been a great factor in changing the entire banking business of the country. Not only has the nation's financial center moved from Wall Street to Main Street; but the banks of the nation have lost much of their former business. The growth of instalment sales, the efficiency of the private finance companies and the granting of Federal loans on real estate have made it unnecessary for the average man longer to go to his local bank to borrow money. Hence, with present restrictions on security purchases by banks, Government bonds are about all that are left for banks to buy. This means that unless there is a marked increase in money rates, there may be a large reduction in the number of national and state banks.

CHAPTER THIRTEEN

What Is the Solution?

"Owe no man anything but to love one another."—*St. Paul*

If courage did not fail me, I should show that the instalment industry may lead to America's downfall. I would demonstrate that the only real assets are children, land and character. I would prove that cities are a curse to every nation; while the desire for ease, which the instalment industry is stimulating, is increasing in the cities and lowering the birth rates. But I will stick to the subject of statistics.

Readers of this book, however, must begin to wonder what the Federal Government can do to check the evils of instalment buying. Let me say that the first step should be to get correct statistics on the amount of instalment business being done. Various figures on retail trade are published each month. These are for the large stores and are supposed to be indicative of the entire country. Actually they cover only about 15% of the total retail sales. The United States is still a nation of small shopkeepers. This 15% should be increased to at least 85%.

IMPORTANT RECOMMENDATIONS

Far more important is it to know what percentage of these sales are for cash and to know the average length of time for which credit has been extended. Figures on collections should also be available. We should know what Main Street is loaning as well as what Wall Street is loaning. This is especially important as the percentage of Main Street loans to the total for the entire country is constantly increasing. Only when such statistics are available can a *start* be made toward checking this economic cancer.

The second step should be to insist upon an adequate differential between sales for cash and sales on time. Everyone admits that the instalment business results in cash buyers paying more than they should for merchandise. Therefore, this differential encourages people to buy on instalments instead of paying cash. Every price tag should have two figures,—one the sales price for cash and the other the sales price for credit. Later, I may go further and say that there should be one other figure, namely, the cost of the goods to the merchant.

VALUE OF EDUCATION

The public should be educated as to the harm one does himself, his family and his nation, by purchasing goods on instalments. Such educational work may be very difficult under a democratic form of government. A dictator may be necessary to put over such a campaign. It would step upon many toes and temporarily hurt many people. However, unless the danger of instalment buying is soon realized, the result may be very serious. The business cannot safely be allowed to increase as it has increased in the past.

Yet, with the three steps: (1) statistics, (2) price differentials, and (3) education—will the problem be solved? I fear not. As I have already stated, the problem fundamentally is one of the spirit. The curse of instalment buying will be eliminated only as the *desires* of people are controlled and directed along saner lines. This requires a faith and self-control which will come about only as the country is swept by a spiritual revival. Statistics, price tags and even education are mere tools.

Statistics, price tags and education, like other tools, are of little value unless people wish to use them. Even then they can be used to upbuild or to destroy according to the purposes, motives and ambitions of those who have these tools. This especially applies to anything so settled and intangible as demand for goods. Even labor leaders have learned that they can force employers to raise prices and can force Congress to shorten hours, but they cannot force the public to buy goods. On the other hand, when the public gets into a buying move, nothing for a time will stop the buying.

This brings me to another matter which has an important bearing on the situation, namely, *the demand for goods*. What creates demand? What satisfies demand? What are the limits to which demand can be stimulated at a profit? What are the true results of advertising—that is, does it really pay? These are vital questions, but many sales experts will tell you that the answers are not known. The entire art of selling and buying *intelligently* is in its infancy. This accounts largely for the unreasonably high cost of distribution.

Research convinces me that the answers to these and similar questions never will be known until the entire problem of distribution is reopened and studied from a spiritual standpoint. From such an analysis, we would learn that the important questions "in the sight of God" probably would not be: *How much did you buy?* or *Did you pay with cash?* Rather: *What did you buy? Was it useful? How have you used it?* This may all be summed up in the super-question of stewardship.

A WORLDWIDE PROBLEM

In addition to instalment purchasing being a spiritual problem, it also is a worldwide problem. Some years ago it gained considerable headway in England. As explained in a previous chapter, it has there been discussed in Parliament as well as in economic circles. From England it spread to the Colonies. It is now increasing throughout all countries. Japan, China and India are getting a taste of this new but dangerous stimulant.

This is another reason why the whole world is heading for inflation and labor trouble. An easy way to sell and buy has been invented. Instalment selling is destined to become as great an international problem as tariffs. Those who first used tariffs greatly benefited therefrom. Then all countries had to follow suit in order to hold their home trade. Finally, when all countries had the same tariffs, all were back to where they started except for the taxes collected.

Until the World War the leading nations were re-tailing on virtually a cash basis. During the War all merchandise was crimped. After the War, other nations saw American and British retail sales increase at a tremendous rate through the stimulus of instalment purchases. It was only natural for other countries to resort to the same stimulant. Every nation is now giving its trade these artificial shots-in-the-arm. The result is labor troubles and inflation.

Can the stimulant now be taken away? In countries which are ruled by dictators, the stimulant can be withheld. Sales can there be put back on a normal basis and the ill effects avoided. I, however, seriously doubt whether democracies can so retrace their steps. Manufacturers, merchants and wage-workers would be apt to wreck any Administration which "took away the baby's bottle." The instalment business has an underlying political significance in the United States, England and France similar to that of the liquor business.

NATURALLY I AM PERSECUTED

Of course, the instalment people violently object to my picture of their industry. They reply that the notes given by purchasers mature and are paid before the goods purchased wear out. Thus the debt is not permanent, but merely a revolving fund. This is largely true. I am not attacking the industry from that standpoint. My claims are: (1) instalment selling is inflationary; (2) instalment selling raises the prices of goods for everybody; (3) instalment selling is a chief cause of radicalism; and (4) instalment selling undermines the character of the people.

After my father died in Gloucester I went down there to clean out his old roll-top desk. At the back of the desk I found a motto: "Debts kill more people than do germs." This motto states in a few words the great harm being done by the instalment business to the morale of the people. Never mind if the grand total of outstanding notes is increasing only slowly, due to their constant retirement. Statistics on vice may show only a small *increase* from year to year. Is that a reason for upholding vice?

The serious fact to consider is the *total* figures for either instalment sales or vice. If the outstanding instalment indebtedness is only $1,000,000,000, it means that our families are constantly under the strain of this indebtedness. Statistics will probably show that these instalment notes always total several times this amount. Furthermore, the very fact that these instalment notes are given for a short time, maturing each month, makes the instalment business even a real factor in keeping the nation upset.

The entire instalment business is unnecessary. People could be taught to save and buy later as easily as to go into debt to buy in advance. It is training people to get into dangerous habits; it is causing the country to run without any reserve; it is forcing business to depend upon artificial stimulation; it is raising havoc with employment and it is undermining the nation's morale. The instalment industry is one potent reason for a nation's being at low ebb spiritually.

NOTE THIS CARTOON

Around New Year's Day in 1938 was published a cartoon showing a father exhibiting a family budget to his wife with the exultant remark:

"We are now entirely out of debt. I have made the last payment on the car; we owe only the doctor, the dentist and a few stores!"

This well illustrates what has happened during the past few years. The pressure of instalment debts has been so great that the average man does not call anything a debt unless he has given a note, secured by mortgage on something tangible. As a result, the instalment business is making our citizens dishonest and unreliable. Those traits of thrift, industry and reliability which created America are fast becoming obsolete. It used to be disgraceful to receive public aid from a city; but now people think it is smart. It used to be dishonest not to pay one's bills; but now "nobody does it."

The whole attitude toward life changed for the worse after the World War. The public thinks it is "good business" to run up as much debt as possible with one doctor, dentist or merchant and then calmly change to another. Entire communities are honeycombed with dishonesty. People fail to realize that a very thin veil separates carelessness from crime. I believe that the sale of automobiles on "easy terms" is in part responsible for the present serious state of the nation's morals. The automobile manufacturers will doubtless blame it on the policies of the Democratic Administration which entered office in 1932. The facts will show, however, that although examples set at Washington doubtless encouraged the decline, yet American morale began to slip before 1932.

WHAT ABOUT CREDIT INSURANCE?

The question arises as to how long the present downward moral trend can continue. Those who think it is smart to "beat the dentist" refer back to the days when men were put in jail for debt. They say that a study of history shows that for over two hundred years the world has been becoming more lenient to debtors.

On the other hand, there must be some end to such a decadent policy. No sound prosperity can be built on a sand foundation. Manufacturers may, once or twice, get by when welching on raw material contracts. Retailers may, for a while, succeed in securing price adjustments by refusing to accept goods which they had definitely ordered. The public can, for a certain time, buy everything on partial payments and then demand Federal aid or higher wages to foot the bills. Right, however, always has won in the end. I am optimistic enough to believe right will this time. "Though the mills of God grind slowly, yet they grind exceeding small."

I feel that this irresponsible attitude has been caused by manufacturers, merchants and others depending upon the laws of averages rather than the laws of God. Statisticians figure from existing records that only a certain percentage of the people mean to be dishonest. They explain to the business interests that, by adding this percentage to the price of the goods, the honest will carry the dishonest.

Hence, there is no attempt to make people honest. Little effort is made to teach decent business morals. Recoverable goods are taken back; but almost never is action taken to enforce the contract. Everyone depends upon the law of averages for protection. Even burglars say it is safer to rob a home which carries burglary insurance. Not only is the family more careless about locking the doors and windows, but the insurance companies are said to need a certain number of burglaries in order to sell burglary insurance.

This brings us to the question of insurance in general. Life insurance causes parents to depend upon the insurance company for old-age protection instead of upon their children. Hence, they give less and less attention to the bringing up of their children. To this extent life insurance may be responsible for the decline in parental authority and the accompanying irresponsibility of modern youth. Everything can now be insured "against." When a package comes from a department store, it often contains a little slip with a number on it. You wonder how the delivery driver can dare to leave the package at your door without getting a receipt. The answer is that every step of the delivery is insured. The sales clerk is insured; the shipping boys are insured; the truck is insured; the driver is insured; and the package is insured. The little slip is the stub of the "insurance policy" which is held by the shipping department of the store!

The insurance industry is a great industry. It is operated scientifically by high-minded men. It is very doubtful, however, whether it is making a better or safer world in which to live. It assumes and thrives upon dishonesty; it does not suppress it. It is very possible that insurance is leading us into a blind alley from which escape may be very difficult.

I may be old-fashioned; but I believe that the only insurance which has stood the test of time is the Ten Commandments. Just now this Code is in the discard. History teaches that this Code has been in the discard before. For a time, substitutes have appeared to be better. In each instance, however, the Ten Commandments have been returned to, dusted off and used once more. I believe the day is coming when the instalment business and perhaps many forms of insurance will be greatly curtailed. Once more we will return to the Ten Commandments based upon thousands of years of experience.

IS ADVERTISING INNOCENT?

This is not a book on advertising. Perhaps the subject should not be brought up even in these last few pages. I must, however, say this much about it. *Advertising has great possibilities for evil as well as for good.* I do not refer now to dishonest advertising. The advertisers themselves can be depended upon to eliminate this form of dishonesty. Neither, at the moment, have I in mind the use of advertising to entice people to buy more liquor, cigarettes, and other things which are generally recognized as harmful. This is a subject which is too large to discuss in these pages. Rather, I have in mind the basic fact that advertising has put too great emphasis on material things and too little on the things of the spirit. Even advertisers will admit that most of these *things* which they advertise do not make people better, healthier or happier. The fact is that in many cases this advertising has resulted in making people less honest, in increasing accidents and in developing unrest and jealousy.

Our old world may be likened to a ship. It is unsafe in the long run for all the passengers and the cargo to be on the same side of the boat. Yet this is the very thing which has been happening since the World War. We have put an undue emphasis on material things. We have gone crazy making merchandise and have neglected making men. Unless our passengers and cargo get redistributed in a more normal way, the ship named *Civilization* is apt to capsize.

The first newspaper was printed in this country in 1704.[1] Very few newspapers existed in any part of the world before that date. In the early days of newspapers, advertising was not considered. Gradually, paid public notices began to creep into the newspapers. We find the notices of public meetings. These notices were paid for by a political party. We find advertisements of steamboat and railroad schedules. All the

---

[1] Disregarding an attempt in 1690 to start a newspaper, of which only one issue was published.

advertisements then had the semblance of news. When the first advertisements of commodities appeared they read:

John Brown & Company Announces

That next week a shipment of lumber is expected to arrive at Long Wharf. It is of spruce and pine of all sizes. It will be reasonably priced.

The advertisements were newsy and truthful.

The newspaper industry had nearly "grown up" before modern advertising was accepted. The bars were let down by the acceptance of patent-medicine advertising. Therefore it will be seen that modern advertising is of comparatively recent origin. Modern advertising started out on the wrong foot. Admittedly most of it is much better in *quality*, as this book is being written, than it was in the gay Nineties or even before. These comments, therefore, are not a criticism of any advertisement *per se*.

The advertising tendency which I fear concerns the *intensity* of modern advertising. In the early newspaper days, the subscription price of the paper was supposed to cover costs and provide a profit. It was never then thought that a *newspaper* would be obliged to depend upon advertising for its very existence. It was never dreamed that the income from advertising would become a factor in determining the editorials and news policies of the *news*papers.

In the meantime, competition for circulation, upon

which the income from advertising depends, has forced expenses to unbelievable heights. To secure advertising, more circulation is needed. To secure more circulation, a larger and more sensational paper is needed. To make such a "bigger" paper, more advertising is necessary. Hence, every newspaper publisher is caught in a vicious circle. When this will end, no one dares to think.

During this same period, the merchants and manufacturers have been subject to a similar vicious circle. To sell more goods, they find it necessary to do more advertising. To do this advertising, they are compelled to get more profits. To get more profits, they are compelled to sell more goods and so it goes. These facts, moreover, apply not only to newspapers, but to magazines, billboards, radio broadcasting and many other forms of advertising which are so severely taxing consumers. Newspapers, merchants and consumers are now much like squirrels chasing one another on a revolving wheel in a cage. Lots of action, but none of them are getting anywhere.

As a final climax to this useless race comes the instalment business and the propaganda behind it. This has had the effect of adding kerosene to a fire already burning dangerously high. Not content to let the squirrels run about the cage chasing one another of their own free will, we spur them on by bait and fear. An artificial stimulant is added to an already dangerous practice.

Let it be repeated. The crime of instalment selling

is not the individual indictments which can be brought against the industry. These may be wrong and harmful, but they are incidental to the basic difficulty. This difficulty is that instalment selling is adding a crowning blow to an already dangerous situation. It is causing this combination of manufacturers, advertisers, merchants and consumers to go more madly after material things to the neglect of the things of the spirit. Yet, in their hearts, the hardest-boiled persons know that *more things do not bring more happiness.*

As a closing thought I quote from an article [1] by my friend Dr. Thomas Nixon Carver, who since 1902 has been professor and professor emeritus of political economy at Harvard University. The day will come when these prophetic words of Professor Carver will be accepted as one of the outstanding principles of economics. I have taken the liberty of printing his final sentence in italics.

"To summarize, consumer credit is not a device which enables consumers indefinitely to buy more than they could buy for cash. During the period while credit is in process of expansion, consumers can buy more than they could for cash. But when credit is no longer expanding, even though it remains unimpaired, they cannot buy any more than they could if they could pay cash and did not have to use their cash to pay for things bought weeks before. When consumer credit begins to contract, and as long as it is in the

[1] From The Annals of The American Academy of Political and Social Science, Philadelphia, March 1938.

process of contraction, consumers cannot buy as much as they could if they had no debts to pay and were able to use their incomes to make cash purchases. *This expansion and contraction of consumer credit makes for economic instability."*

ADDENDA

Those who have read the manuscript for this book say:

"All your criticisms may be true but you offer little that is constructive. What would you recommend in place of existing stimulants? Something must be done to reduce unemployment."

The purpose of these short addenda is to answer this question. My recommendations are as follows:

(1) Cease trying to fix the prices of labor, or commodities. All such attempts lead directly to more unemployment. This applies to labor unions, farm organizations and business corporations. All forms of monopolies increase unemployment. Hence price fixing of all kinds should be stamped out as harmful to the nation as a whole. Politicians talk about "overproduction." It is true that certain industries can suffer from overproduction when they get out of line. There, however, can be no overproduction in all industries. Only as more is produced is there more to divide. The standard of living can be raised only through greater production—never by restrictive production.

(2) Amend the Securities Exchange Act and also Federal Tax legislation so as to encourage—instead of discourage—new enterprises. Differentiate between speculation in new risks from speculation in outstanding securities. If more receipts are needed by the Federal Government after eliminating restrictive profit taxes, put a special tax on Trust Funds. Money in Trust Funds is "dead" money. It is invested only in long-established industries and never takes a risk. As Trust Funds increase, unemployment likewise increases. The tremendous decline in new stock issues caused

247

by unwise security and tax legislation is responsible for much of the unemployment.

(3) Preach the importance of self-dependence. Our Federal and State governments are engaged in all other kinds of propaganda and so-called "educational" work. Most of such efforts result in adding to the unemployed. They are fitting men and women to seek positions in the more crowded occupations. Women have entered industry to stay; but if so, men must be taught to do housework and bring up children. It is dangerous to interfere with the *balance* of nature. We cannot let people starve; but we can put a social and family stigma upon the acceptance of relief. Civilization has depended upon such a stigma for centuries. Its sudden removal has been a primary cause for unemployment.

(4) Cut out politics for four or eight years. Leaders of both great political parties agree that the above program would do much to eliminate abnormal unemployment. They however add that it would be suicidal for either the Democrats or the Republicans to advocate independently such a program. This means that the sensible people of both parties should temporarily unite in this emergency. Let us follow England by having a coalition government until we get back to normal and natural methods of living. Probably the most practical way of accomplishing this would be for the Republicans to nominate in 1940 a sensible Democrat. There are several such in our United States Senate.

———

The Roosevelt Administration has done many worth-while things. In many ways it has made a better nation. Its attempts to change human nature and set aside natural laws have resulted in much unnecessary unemployment. Let us continue the good legislation and repeal the bad. This will restore confidence both in the minds of labor and management. Prosperity of a substantial form will then return.

THE END

GETTING AND SPENDING:
The Consumer's Dilemma
An Arno Press Collection

Babson, Roger W[ard]. **The Folly of Instalment Buying.** 1938

Bauer, John. **Effective Regulation of Public Utilities.** 1925

Beckman, Theodore N. and Herman C. Nolen. **The Chain Store Problem.** 1938

Berridge, William A., Emma A. Winslow and Richard A. Flinn. **Purchasing Power of the Consumer.** 1925

Borden, Neil H. **The Economic Effects of Advertising.** 1942

Borsodi, Ralph. **The Distribution Age.** 1927

Brainerd, J. G[rist], editor. **The Ultimate Consumer.** 1934

Carson, Gerald. **Cornflake Crusade.** [1957]

Cassels, John M[acIntyre]. **A Study of Fluid Milk Prices.** 1937

Caveat Emptor. 1976

Cherington, Paul Terry. **Advertising as a Business Force.** 1913

Clark, Evans. **Financing the Consumer.** 1933

Cook, James. **Remedies and Rackets:** The Truth About Patent Medicines Today. [1958]

Cover, John H[igson]. **Neighborhood Distribution and Consumption of Meat in Pittsburgh.** [1932]

Federal Trade Commission. **Chain Stores.** 1933

Ferber, Robert and Hugh G. Wales, editors. **Motivation and Market Behavior.** 1958

For Richer or Poorer. 1976

Grether, Ewald T. **Price Control Under Fair Trade Legislation.** 1939

Harding, T. Swann. **The Popular Practice of Fraud.** 1935

Haring, Albert. **Retail Price Cutting and Its Control by Manufacturers.** [1935]

Harris, Emerson P[itt]. **Co-operation:** The Hope of the Consumer. 1918

Hoyt, Elizabeth Ellis. **The Consumption of Wealth.** 1928

Kallen, Horace M[eyer]. **The Decline and Rise of the Consumer.** 1936

Kallet, Arthur and F. J. Schlink. **100,000,000 Guinea Pigs:** Dangers in Everyday Foods, Drugs, and Cosmetics. 1933

Kyrk, Hazel. **A Theory of Consumption.** [1923]

Laird, Donald A[nderson]. **What Makes People Buy.** 1935

Lamb, Ruth deForest. **American Chamber of Horrors:** The Truth About Food and Drugs. [1936]

Lambert, I[saac] E. **The Public Accepts:** Stories Behind Famous Trade-Marks, Names, and Slogans. [1941]

Larrabee, Carroll B. **How to Package for Profit.** 1935

Lough, William H. **High-Level Consumption.** 1935

Lyon, Leverett S[amuel]. **Hand-to-Mouth Buying.** 1929

Means, Gardiner C. **Pricing Power and the Public Interest.** [1962]

Norris, Ruby Turner. **The Theory of Consumer's Demand.** 1952

Nourse, Edwin G. **Price Making in a Democracy.** 1944

Nystrom, Paul H[enry]. **Economic Principles of Consumption.** [1929]

Pancoast, Chalmers Lowell. **Trail Blazers of Advertising.** 1926

Pasdermadjian, H[rant]. **The Department Store.** 1954

Pease, Otis. **The Responsibilities of American Advertising.** 1958

Peixotto, Jessica B[lanche]. **Getting and Spending at the Professional Standard of Living.** 1927

Radin, Max. **The Lawful Pursuit of Gain.** 1931

Reid, Margaret G. **Consumers and the Market.** 1947

Rheinstrom, Carroll. **Psyching the Ads.** [1929]

Rorty, James. **Our Master's Voice:** Advertising. [1934]

Schlink, F. J. **Eat, Drink and Be Wary.** [1935]

Seldin, Joseph J. **The Golden Fleece:** Selling the Good Life to Americans. [1963]

Sheldon, Roy and Egmont Arens. **Consumer Engineering.** 1932

Stewart, Paul W. and J. Frederic Dewhurst. **Does Distribution Cost Too Much?** 1939

Thompson, Carl D. **Confessions of the Power Trust.** 1932

U. S. National Commission on Food Marketing. **Food From Farmer to Consumer.** 1966

U. S. Senate Subcommittee on Anti-Trust and Monopoly of the Committee on the Judiciary. **Administered Prices.** 1963

Waite, Warren C[leland] and Ralph Cassady, Jr. **The Consumer and the Economic Order.** 1939

Washburn, Robert Collyer. **The Life and Times of Lydia E. Pinkham.** 1931

Wiley, Harvey W[ashington]. **The History of a Crime Against the Food Law.** [1929]

Wright, Richardson [Little]. **Hawkers and Walkers in Early America.** 1927

Zimmerman, Carle C[lark]. **Consumption and Standards of Living.** 1936